GOING ON TO
SOLIDS

GOING ON TO SOLIDS

Feeding baby: from 4 months

by

Jenny Kinman

PAPERFRONTS

Typeset in 10/11pt Times by County Typesetters,
Margate, Kent.

Made and Printed in Great Britain by Clays Ltd.,
St Ives plc.

CONTENTS

CHAPTER   PAGE

PART ONE – ESSENTIAL READING

1   Nutrition   9
2   First Tastes   17
3   Establishing Solids   25
4   Equipment   40
5   Food Handling and Storage   47
6   Getting Organised   62

PART TWO – RECIPES FOR BEGINNERS
(from around 4 months)

7   Cereal, Fruit and Vegetable Purées   69

PART THREE – RECIPES FOR OLD HANDS
(6 months onwards)

8   Meat, Fish, Egg and Dairy Food Purées   97
9   Breakfast Ideas   104
10 Simple Soups   109
11 Egg Dishes   117
12 Cheese Dishes   122
13 Fish Dishes   130
14 Meat Dishes   139
15 Vegetable Dishes   151
16 Rice and Pasta Dishes   160
17 Delicious Desserts   168
18 Beverages   176
19 Finger Foods   181
    Index   186

DEDICATION

To Ian, James, Charlotte and Alexandra.
More than words can say . . .

PART ONE

ESSENTIAL READING

I would like to thank Karen Ross, hospital dietician, for checking through the manuscript and for her helpful advice.

1. NUTRITION

This chapter outlines the general principles of good nutrition. A basic understanding of this subject will help you ensure that your baby has a well-balanced diet, supplying all the essential nutrients needed for good health. Details of how to plan a balanced *daily* menu are given in the food groups chart in Chapter Three.

What is nutrition?
Nutrition is the study of *food*.

Food is any solid or liquid which when consumed can provide:
- Energy;
- Material for growth, repair and reproduction; or
- Substances which regulate the production of energy, or processes of growth and repair.

The components of food which have the above functions are called *nutrients*.

The *nutrients* present in food are: carbohydrates; fats; proteins; vitamins; and minerals.

Other constituents of food are: water; dietary fibre; and

natural flavours and colours, which give foods their various tastes and characteristics.

What are calories?
Calories are measures of the energy value of food. Energy is provided by fats, proteins, and carbohydrates, but not from minerals, vitamins and water, which do not contain any calories.

Energy is needed to perform muscular work, maintain body temperature and regulate bodily processes, e.g. breathing.

Foods largely composed of water, e.g. fruit and vegetables, contain little fat, protein or carbohydrate and, therefore, few calories. Fat contains more than twice as much energy as the same weight of carbohydrate or protein.

What are carbohydrates?
Carbohydrates take the form of sugars, starches, and cellulose which are all compounds of carbon, hydrogen, and oxygen.

Sugars can be divided into two main groups:

1. Monosaccharides (simple sugars) i.e. glucose, fructose, and galactose; and
2. Disaccharides (two monosaccharides linked together) i.e. sucrose, maltose, and lactose.

Starches (polysaccharides) are variably composed of hundreds or thousands of joined glucose units.

Cellulose is also a polysaccharide composed of many thousands of glucose units.

Only simple sugars can be absorbed by the body in their natural form. Complex sugars and starches must be converted into glucose before they can be used. Cellulose is completely indigestible to man. It is his main source of dietary fibre.

What do carbohydrates do?
Sugars and starches are the body's main source of energy.

Fibre is necessary for the proper functioning of the digestion.

Where are carbohydrates found?

Natural sugars can be found in: fruit; fruit juices; vegetables; vegetable juices; honey; unrefined sugars; and milk.

Natural starches are available in such foods as: wholegrain cereals and cereal products; e.g. wholemeal flour, wholemeal bread and brown rice; some vegetables: e.g. yams, potatoes, dried beans and peas; and bananas.

Natural carbohydrates should be distinguished from processed carbohydrates, i.e.:

1. Refined sugars (white or brown) and foods containing them, e.g. sweet pastries, cakes, biscuits, confectionery and soft drinks; and
2. Refined cereals and cereal products including: white flour, white bread and white rice; cakes, biscuits; and pastries.

Only natural carbohydrates contain their full complement of vitamins, minerals and fibre. Processing leaves refined carbohydrates with a reduced nutritive value, providing mainly energy. Babies should get a combination of natural carbohydrates and the more beneficial refined carbohydrates such as refined baby cereals, which have been reinforced with vitamins and minerals to make them more nutritious.

What are fats?

Fats are compounds of carbon, hydrogen and oxygen, but the proportion of oxygen is lower than that in carbohydrates. They contain three types of fatty acid:

1. Saturated fatty acids;
2. Polyunsaturated fatty acids, three of which are known as 'essential fatty acids', because they are required in small quantities for good health, but cannot be manufactured by the body; and
3. Monounsaturated fatty acids.

It is the varying proportions in which these fatty acids are present which determine the chemical and physical properties of each fat. Vegetable oils, which contain large amounts of polyunsaturated fatty acids, are liquid at room temperature. Animal fats, e.g. lard and butter, which have a greater quantity of saturated fatty acids, are solid at room temperature.

Where are fats found?
There are two main sources of fats:

- Vegetable sources including: vegetable oils; margarine; and nuts; and
- Animal sources such as: eggs; dairy foods; red meat; fatty fish; and lard.

What do fats do?
Fats provide a concentrated source of energy. Stored fat prevents excessive loss of body heat and protects and insulates vital organs.

What are proteins?
Proteins consist of chains of hundreds or thousands of amino acids. About 20 different amino acids are used by the body. Eight (nine for children) are known as essential amino acids, because they cannot be made by the body and must be provided by the diet. The remaining non-essential amino acids are so described because they can be made by the body from excesses of certain other amino acids in the diet.

What do proteins do?
Proteins are essential for the growth and repair of the body, with any excess being used to provide energy.

Where are proteins found?
Complete proteins, which contain all the essential amino acids, are found in: meat; fish; dairy produce; and soya beans.
   Incomplete proteins which are lacking in one or more of the essential amino acids are found in: wholegrain cereals and

cereal products: e.g. wholemeal flour, wholemeal bread and brown rice; dried beans and peas; and nuts.

Some incomplete protein foods can be combined to provide complete protein, such as wholegrain cereals and beans (e.g. beans on toast), and wholegrain cereals and nuts (e.g. peanut butter sandwiches). This is especially important in vegetarian families.

What are vitamins, where are they found and what do they do?

Vitamins are small substances found in food, which take various chemical forms. They are necessary for growth and all bodily functions.

Vitamins are either:
- water-soluble (vitamins C and B complex); or
- fat-soluble (vitamins A, D, E and K).

Water-soluble vitamins cannot be stored by the body, so foods containing them should be eaten every day. They are easily lost during cooking and should be eaten raw, if possible.

Fat-soluble vitamins can be stored by the body, so daily consumption is not so essential. They are more stable than water-soluble vitamins and are not usually destroyed by heat.

Vitamin A is essential for vision in dim light, for growth, for healthy skin and maintenance of surface tissues, especially those which excrete mucus. Good sources include: fish liver oils; meat, especially liver and kidney; margarine; eggs; and dairy produce (excluding skimmed milk and low-fat yoghurt, unless fortified). Some fruits and vegetables such as carrots, spinach, sweet potatoes, apricots, watercress, mangoes and tomatoes contain a substance called 'carotene' which can be converted by the body into retinol (vitamin A).

Vitamin B (complex) includes: vitamin B_1 (thiamin); vitamin B_2 (riboflavin); niacin; vitamin B_6 (pyridoxine); vitamin B_{12}; folic acid; pantothenic acid; and biotin. They are essential for the utilisation of energy from food, for the promotion of growth, as an aid to digestion and to keep the nervous system in good working order. Meat, fish, eggs, dairy produce, fruit, vegetables, nuts, wholegrain cereals and cereal products (such as wholemeal flour, wholemeal bread and brown rice) and yeast extract are all good sources of the B vitamins.

Vitamin C (ascorbic acid) is necessary for the maintenance of healthy tissues, normal growth, healing of wounds and the prevention of scurvy. It is found mainly in such foods as: vegetables including broccoli, potatoes, green peppers and sprouts; most fruit especially blackcurrants and citrus fruits. Smaller quantities are also available in milk and liver.

Vitamin D is vitally important to the young infant because it is essential for proper bone formation. It is not widely available in foods, and supplements may be necessary. Good sources include: fish liver oils and oily fish. Eggs, margarine and dairy produce (excluding skimmed milk and low-fat yoghurt unless fortified) contain smaller amounts. Vitamin D can also be obtained through the action of sunlight on the skin which is the most important source for most people.

Vitamin E plays an important role in cell structure. It is common in most foods, the richest sources being: vegetable oils; wholegrain cereals and cereal products including wholemeal flour, wholemeal bread and brown rice; eggs; animal fats; and meat.

Vitamin K assists in the normal clotting of blood and is found in most vegetables and wholegrain cereals.

What are minerals, what do they do and where are they found?

Minerals are naturally occurring inorganic substances. Most can be detected in the body, but only about fifteen are known to be essential. They must be derived from food.

The seven minerals most needed in the diet are:

1. Iron;
2. Calcium;
3. Phosphorous;
4. Magnesium;
5. Sodium;

6. Chlorine; and
7. Potassium.

The following minerals are required in much smaller quantities and are known as 'trace elements':

- Cobalt;
- Copper;
- Chromium;
- Fluorine;
- Iodine;
- Manganese;
- Selenium; and
- Zinc.

Iron forms part of the haemoglobin in the blood which is essential for the transportation of oxygen around the body. Good sources include: cocoa and carob powder; meat especially liver and kidney; dried fruits e.g. apricots; wholegrain cereals and cereal products such as wholemeal flour, wholemeal bread and brown rice; eggs; watercress; dried beans, peas and lentils; and green leafy vegetables e.g. spinach.

Calcium is needed for strong bones, healthy teeth, proper functioning of the heart and nerves, and normal clotting of blood. It is found mainly in such foods as: dairy produce; tinned fish, e.g. sardines and salmon where the bones are eaten; and in smaller amounts in dried fruit; eggs; and some green vegetables, e.g. broccoli and cabbage.

Phosphorous is required for strong bones and teeth and to enable food energy to be utilised by the body. Yeast extract (e.g. Marmite), cheese, nuts, eggs, wholegrain cereals and cereal products (e.g. wholemeal flour, wholemeal bread and brown rice), fish, poultry, meat and milk are all good sources of this mineral.

Magnesium is essential for healthy bones and body tissues, and for the release of energy during metabolism. It is available from: yeast extract, e.g. Marmite; nuts; wholegrain cereals and cereal products; dairy foods; fish; meat; and some vegetables; e.g. cabbage and potatoes.

Sodium and chlorine (more commonly known as sodium chloride or salt) are a vital element of all body fluids. They help maintain the water balance of the body and proper muscle and nerve activity. Sufficient salt is present to a varying extent in all foods without any added salt being required.

Potassium is present in all body cells and has similar functions to sodium chloride. Good sources include: dried fruit, e.g. sultanas; some vegetables, e.g. potatoes and cauliflower; some fruits including bananas, mangoes, oranges, peaches and tomatoes; meat; fish; and wholegrain cereals and cereal products.

2. FIRST TASTES

What is weaning?
Weaning is the process of gradually replacing milk by solid foods.

Why do I need to wean baby onto solid foods?
Your baby needs to be weaned onto solid foods:

- For the extra calories they will provide. As baby grows older, milk alone will not supply sufficient energy to meet his requirements;

- For the valuable nutrients they will give him. Milk is very low in some of these, for example, iron. Baby needs solid foods to ensure he continues to get all the nutrients necessary for good health; and

- For social reasons. Baby will want to join in with what the rest of the family are doing, including their eating habits.

How do I know when to start offering baby solid foods?
It is best to offer solid foods *just before* baby really starts to need them.

This is when he begins to demand more frequent feeds, after having been satisfied by the same number for some time, or wants more milk than usual at each feed.

Generally this happens at around four months. However, all babies are individuals; some may need to start solid food earlier than this, some later. If baby is happy on milk only, there is no harm in waiting until five to six months. On the other hand, if you want baby to start solid foods before the age of four months, you should discuss it with your doctor or health visitor first. They may want you to wait a while if possible. Starting mixed feeding too early can put unnecessary strain on baby's immature digestive system.

Also consult the doctor before offering solid foods to baby if there is a *strong family history of allergy*. He may advise you to avoid certain foods which are known to cause allergies, e.g. egg whites, until baby is older.

What types of food should I offer to baby?
From around four months you may offer:

1. Cereal purées, fruit purées and vegetable purées. See the recipes for beginners given in Part II of this book. You do not have to prepare all the purées exactly as instructed. For example, if you want to give baby carrot purée, and you are cooking carrots for the rest of the family anyway, just allow a little extra for baby. But remove his portion before adding any salt.

2. Any of the commercially-prepared foods for babies, e.g. baby rice, dinners, desserts, etc., provided baby is old enough for them according to the manufacturer's directions.

(Homemade dishes containing meat, fish, eggs and dairy foods can be gradually introduced from the age of six months. Part III of this book includes full instructions on how to prepare these foods as purées and as part of combination dishes.)

Whichever solids you decide to offer, remember to try only one new food at a time, for three or four days, to give baby a

chance to grow to like it, before offering another food. It may
take time for him to become accustomed to a new taste.

How much food should I give baby?
Only offer a small amount to begin with, about a teaspoonful
at first, which you can increase a little each day.

   Once baby is getting used to solids, you can let him be the
guide as to how much he wants to eat. Watch out though.
Babies do sometimes go overboard for certain foods and try
to eat far more than seems reasonable. Pear purée was my
first-born's particular weakness and at four months he was
quite put out by the fact that I wanted to limit him to one pear
at a time!

How often should I give baby solid foods?
To begin with, offer baby solid food once a day. Over the next
few weeks this can be gradually increased to three or four
times a day. The speed at which you can increase the
frequency of baby's solid feeds will depend very much on
baby's appetite and how quickly he becomes accustomed to
eating the food.

   There is a sample weaning guide in the next chapter (page
26) which shows how baby can progress from being given his
first taste of solid food on to a completely adult-style diet. No
baby would follow the guide exactly, but it will give you some
idea of average progress.

When is the best time to give baby his solid foods?
Choose the time that suits your baby. Time of day is not
important at this stage, so long as baby is alert and happy.
   Offer baby his solid food either:

1. Halfway through a feed. Let baby have half his milk from
   his bottle (or feed from one breast only), then offer the
   solid food before letting him finish up with as much milk
   as he wants, or;

2. After he has finished his feed as normal, if he will not be
   too full by then.

Prepare the dish in advance and have it next to you, ready to give to baby at the right moment. This is especially important if you opt for plan 1 as any delay may cause him to think that the feeding session has ended and make him fight for the rest of his milk, so rejecting any other food you offer without even trying it.

Keep experimenting until you know which method suits your baby best. Make sure it suits *you* as well.

Do not pick a time when:

He is frantically hungry for his milk feed. Milk will be the only thing he expects or wants. Mummy trying to place an unknown solid substance between his lips will only confuse and frustrate him;

He is tired. Tired babies are not interested in new experiences, they only want to sleep;

He is ill. This may sound obvious but it is probably best if you do not even, for example, offer baby his first taste of solid food just as he is getting over a cold. If his nose is still a little blocked, he will be having enough trouble drinking his milk and may not feel like tackling solid food as well. Furthermore, supposing baby is put off solid foods through being ill, his disinterest may continue even after he has completely recovered, if he remembers the process of trying to eat as being a chore;

He is full up after a milk feed. If he is not at all hungry, he may agree to taste the food but is unlikely to swallow it!

How should I start offering baby solid foods?

Either sit him up on your lap, or put him in a baby-chair. Put a bib on him. Have plenty of kitchen roll ready, it is amazing how much mess one little baby can make with a few teaspoonfuls of food!

Next, carefully place a tiny amount of food on the end of a very small shallow spoon (such as a salt-spoon). Alternatively, if baby seems to prefer it, you could dip a *clean* finger into the food and let him suck the food off – he may find this way easier at first.

When you have your loaded spoon or finger at the ready, place the food just between baby's lips, then wait for him to suck the food off. Be patient. Babies are very slow eaters! Baby has to learn how to get the food from the front of his mouth to the back and down his throat. If he likes the taste of it, he will probably suck some of it into his mouth and swallow it. It may appear that all the food just oozes back out onto his chin, but some probably goes down too. So do not be deceived. Just scrape any that oozes out straight back into his mouth again.

Keep going until either all the food has gone, or baby *clearly* indicates that he has had enough, for example, by flatly refusing to open his mouth, turning his head away completely or beginning to cry. If baby's message is unclear, patience combined with a slower pace or a little gentle coaxing may well do the trick. Never try to force baby to eat if he *really* does not want to. Baby will only learn to enjoy his food if he can decide for himself, how much, how quickly, and what he will eat.

Are there any foods which I should not give to baby?
Most foods, if prepared in a suitable manner, for example, without the addition of too much fat, can be offered to a baby to try. However the following are best avoided:

1. Foods to which salt has been added. Baby will obtain enough salt from his diet naturally, without being given any extra   too much salt puts an unnecessary strain on baby's immature kidneys.

2. Foods to which spices have been added. These can be *gradually* introduced from the age of six months.

3. Foods to which sugar has been added, or very sugary foods in general (including sugary drinks). The exceptions would be where the food is too tart otherwise, for

example, stewed cooking apples, or too bland, for example, porridge. Always add the minimum amount necessary and use honey or unrefined sugars if possible. Too much very sweet food encourages a sweet tooth and promotes tooth decay.

4. Household milk before the age of six months. Give breast milk and/or infant formula only before this age.

5. Fried foods, especially deep fried foods.

6. Tea, coffee, or alcohol. These are all drugs. An occasional weak cup of tea or coffee would do no harm to an older child.

Generally you should use as much fresh food as possible when preparing meals for your baby. This will help you to avoid giving too many unnecessary additives which may be present in commercially-packaged foods (except baby foods which are not allowed to contain any by law).

Remember too that tap water should be boiled first for babies under six months.

How can I ensure that baby enjoys the food I give him?
Baby probably won't enjoy every food you give him. Food that he loves at four months may be refused at one year, and vice versa, but if you follow the guidelines below you should cut rejections to a minimum.

1. Be positive. Try not to appear anxious when you offer food. Service should be with a smile. If you are relaxed, baby will probably relax also. If you are anxious, you may transmit this feeling and baby will not be so keen to eat his food. If baby does reject what you have offered to him, take it away with a smile (no matter how you may be feeling inside!) and try to forget about it. There are so many different foods a baby can eat, it does not matter that he will not take a few of them.

2. Always try to ensure that the food is neither too hot nor too cold. All babies will be put off eating if they are offered food that is too hot. Some babies will tolerate colder food than others, perhaps even straight out of the refrigerator. However, most babies like their food to be at room temperature, or lukewarm if you are serving a 'hot meal'.

3. Ensure that you are using the right technique to feed your baby, as explained on page 20. Never try to place food straight into the back of baby's mouth in the hope that it will help him to swallow the food. This is more likely to frighten baby into thinking he is going to choke, and may put him off solid foods.

4. Always ensure that the food is of the right consistency. The first purées that you offer should be free from all lumps, the consistency of thin cream. If the purée is too thick, or lumpy, baby will probably be put off by the texture, even if he liked the taste.

5. Choose a good time to offer baby his first taste of solid food, as explained on page 19.

6. Try to remove any distractions, such as mobiles, pets, other children, daddy, etc., which may be more interesting at this early stage than the strange substances which you want baby to swallow!

What should I do if baby rejects the food I give him?
If you have followed my advice, then the most likely reason for baby's rejection of his food is, quite simply, that he does not like the taste of it. If this happens:

Respect his judgment and do not offer any more of the same food. While baby is still inexperienced in the art of eating, do not offer any other food at the same sitting either. He will be expecting a repeat of the food which he does not like, so will probably reject the new food also, without even trying it. (When baby is a little older he may be prepared to give you a 'second chance', if your first offering has not come up to his expectations!) So wait several hours or until the next day before offering a different food. Once you hit on something baby loves, he will become more keen to eat from a spoon and may well surprise you by devouring the original rejected food with relish in one or two weeks' time.

If you try three or four times, and baby still does not seem interested in anything, wait for a few days before trying again.

If baby still does not seem interested, but is otherwise contented and gaining weight, etc., it is most likely that he is still getting all he requires from his milk and is not quite ready for solid food. Wait a couple of weeks before trying again.

If at any time baby's behaviour causes real concern, consult your doctor, just in case the reason for the rejection of solid foods is due to a condition which requires treatment.

3. ESTABLISHING SOLIDS

Having tried solids for the first few times how do I progress?
The weaning guide below shows how the average baby can
progress from a milk-only-diet to a regular eating pattern of
three main meals per day.

Notes to the guide
1. In the guide, solid feeding commences at four months. If
   your baby needs to start earlier or later than this you will
   have to alter the ages accordingly.

2. For simplicity it is assumed that, to begin with, baby has
   five milk feeds per day (6 am, 10 am, 2 pm, 6 pm and
   10 pm). If your baby is demand-fed more often than this,
   fit in the solids at the feed which is nearest the
   recommended time. As baby progresses, you will probably
   find that the extra calories provided by his solid food will
   enable him to need less frequent feeds, until he is having
   five per day at roughly the times given.

3. The order in which the guide introduces different types of
   foods is not important. You can vary this if you want to.

4. No specific mention is made of drinks in-between meals, so do not forget to offer these whenever you think baby may be thirsty. You can offer fruit juice which is best diluted at least fifty/fifty with water (previously boiled for babies under six months) or any of the commercially-prepared drinks for babies. From six months, baby can start having household milk to drink (ask your health visitor whether the milk should be boiled first). See Chapter 18 on beverages for some more unusual ideas.

5. Remember this is only a guide and is not meant to be rigidly adhered to. Your baby is the only one who can really tell you what food he likes and how he would like it prepared.

Stage one
Age four months
All purées should be smooth and the consistency of very thin cream.

Early morning (6 am)
Baby will not want to miss his first and most important feed of the day so breast or bottle feed as usual.

Breakfast (10 am)
Come armed to the second feed of the day with one or two teaspoons of fruit purée (see page 70 for recipes) and put it where baby can see it while he is having his milk feed. (This is important because you are hoping that in a few weeks' time baby will be so excited at the sight of his solid food he will want to have that first.) Breast or bottle feed baby first, or adopt the half-way system, then offer the fruit purée.

Continue to offer a gradually increasing quantity of your chosen purée at the same time for three to four days, then repeat the process with a different fruit. Keep going until baby has sampled as many varieties as possible. If baby refuses any fruit completely, offer another the next day and try the rejected purée again in a couple of weeks.

Dinner (2 pm)
Breast or bottle feed.

Tea (6 pm)
Breast or bottle feed.

Evening (10 pm)
Breast or bottle feed.

Stage two
Age four and three-quarter months
All purées should be smooth and the consistency of thin cream.

Early morning (6 am)
Although baby will be beginning to enjoy his solid food, he will still want his milk feed first in the morning, so breast or bottle feed as usual.

Breakfast (10 am)
Baby will not be so eager for milk as he was at 6 am and may get quite excited at the sight of one of his fruit purées, thus indicating to you that he would like that first, and milk afterwards. Even if you see no outward signs of enthusiasm, try giving his solids first and see what happens. If he starts to fight for his milk feed, give him some or all of that before the purée for a few more days then try again.

Dinner (2 pm)
If baby happily took his solids first at 10 am, let him try one or two teaspoons of vegetable purée (see page 82 for recipes) before the 2 pm feed.

Continue to offer a gradually increasing quantity of your chosen purée at the same time for three to four days, then repeat the process with a different vegetable. Keep going until baby has sampled as many varieties as possible. If baby refuses any vegetable completely, offer another the next day and try the rejected purée again in a couple of weeks.

Tea (6 pm)
Breast or bottle feed.

Evening (10 pm)
Breast or bottle feed.

Stage three
Age five and a half months
All purées should be smooth and the consistency of medium cream.

Early morning (6 am)
Breast or bottle feed.

Breakfast (10 am)
Fruit purée followed by breast or bottle feed.

Dinner (2 pm)
Vegetable purée followed by breast or bottle feed.

Tea (6 pm)
If baby is quite happily taking his solids first at breakfast and dinner, let him try one or two teaspoons of cereal purée (see page 70 for recipe, or use one of the proprietary brands, e.g. baby rice) before the 6 pm feed.

Continue to offer a gradually increasing quantity of your chosen purée at the same time for three or four days, then repeat the process with a different cereal. Keep going until baby has sampled as many varieties as possible. If baby refuses any purée completely, offer another the next day and try the rejected purée again in a couple of weeks.

Evening (10 pm)
Breast or bottle feed.

Stage four
Age six to seven months

Very soft foods, for example, bananas, potatoes and white fish, need only be roughly mashed. All other foods should be smoothly puréed to the consistency of thick cream.

Early morning (6 am)
Breast or bottle feed.

Breakfast (10 am)
Cereal purée or breakfast idea from Chapter 9 then breast or bottle feed.

Dinner (2 pm)
One of the recipes from Chapters 10 to 16 (inclusive). Then, unless baby indicates that he wants his usual breast or bottle feed, offer him a drink from a bottle or cup instead e.g. household milk, fruit juice and water, or one of the beverages from Chapter 18. If he starts to fight for his milk feed, give that instead for a few more days then try again. Once baby drops a feed he will not normally want it back later, except in times of stress or during an illness when he may lose interest in some or all of his solid foods and want to return to the security of sucking milk. If this happens, don't offer solid foods until the crisis has passed, or only offer those which baby has shown he really enjoys, then pick up from where you left off when baby has recovered.

Tea (6 pm)
Another recipe from Chapters 10 to 16 (inclusive) or cereal if not given at breakfast.

Evening (10 pm)
Breast or bottle feed.

Stage five
Age seven to eight months
Hard foods such as apple and celery will still need to be finely puréed or grated. Chewy foods such as meat will still need to be puréed but to a slightly coarser consistency than before.

Soft foods (including finger foods) need not be puréed and can be given in bite-size pieces for baby to chew.

Early morning (6 am)
If baby is rising early, offer him a drink from a bottle or a cup instead of the usual milk feed. If he starts to fight for his milk give him that instead for a few more days and then try again. Once baby drops the first feed of the day breakfast will have to be brought forward (whether or not he continues to have a drink first thing in the morning), so too will dinner and tea.

Breakfast (8 am – 10 am)
Cereal or breakfast idea from Chapter 9 followed by a drink.

Dinner (12 noon – 2 pm)
One of the recipes from Chapters 10 to 16 (inclusive). Fruit or one of the dessert ideas from Chapter 17 if baby's appetite demands it. Drink.

Tea (4 – 6 pm)
Sandwich or other finger food from Chapter 19, or cereal if not given at breakfast. Fruit or dessert if baby's appetite demands it. Drink.

Evening (10 pm)
Breast or bottle feed.

Stage Six
Eight to nine months
Hard foods should be coarsely puréed or grated. Chewy foods can be coarsely puréed or very finely chopped. Soft foods (including finger foods) can continue to be given in bite-size pieces for baby to chew.

Early morning
Drink if necessary.

Breakfast (8 – 9 am)
Cereal or breakfast idea from Chapter 9 followed by a drink.

Dinner (12 – 1 pm)
One of the recipes from Chapters 10 to 16 (inclusive). Fruit or dessert if baby's appetite demands it. Drink.

Tea (4 – 5 pm)
Finger food, or cereal if not given at breakfast. Fruit or dessert if baby's appetite demands it. Drink.

Before bedtime
Unless baby indicates that he wants his milk feed, offer him a drink from a bottle or a cup instead. If he starts to fight for his milk, give him that instead for a few more days then try again.

Stage seven
Nine to twelve months
Hard foods should still be coarsely grated or puréed (this will have to continue until baby has enough teeth to chew them properly to avoid the possibility of him choking by trying to swallow them in lumps). All other spoon-fed foods can be given in bite-size pieces, except possibly for chewy foods which may still have to be finely chopped or coarsely puréed if baby does not like eating them in bigger lumps. Finger foods can be given in whatever size pieces baby can manage.

Early morning
Drink if necessary.

Breakfast (8 – 9 am)
Cereal or breakfast idea from Chapter 9. Drink.

Dinner (12 – 1 pm)
One of the recipes from Chapters 10 to 16 inclusive. Fruit or dessert if baby's appetite demands it. Drink.

Tea (4 – 5 pm)
Finger food, or cereal if not given at breakfast. Fruit or dessert idea if baby's appetite demands it. Drink.

Before bedtime
Drink.

By the time baby is between nine and twelve months old you will probably have weaned him completely. Some breast-feeding mothers may find that they are still giving baby the last feed of the day. It is all right to continue this practice for many more months, providing you are happy to do so.

How can I ensure that baby is having a well-balanced diet?
Once baby is weaned onto solid food it is very important to ensure that he is getting all the nutrients required for good health. The food groups chart below shows how this can be achieved.

Notes to the food groups chart
1. Include at least one food from each group daily.
2. Try not to serve the same food more than once a day.
3. Vary what you choose daily.
4. Vegetarians should increase their intake of groups 1 and 5 foods to compensate for their lack of group 4 foods.
5. Fats have not been mentioned separately as babies' small requirements are satisfied naturally in a well-balanced diet, e.g. by butter used in cooking or in sandwiches etc.

GROUP	TYPE OF FOOD	WHAT THEY PROVIDE
Group one	Cereals and cereal products such as wholemeal bread and pasta. Pulses and nuts.	Protein, carbohydrates, minerals, vitamins B (complex) and E.
Group two	Fruit, e.g. apples, apricots, bananas, oranges, mangoes, melons, peaches, pears, plums.	Carbohydrates. Minerals especially iron (dried fruit) and potassium. Vitamins A (yellow/orange-coloured fruits), B

GROUP	TYPE OF FOOD	WHAT THEY PROVIDE
		(complex) and C (especially black-currants, strawberries and citrus fruits). Fibre.
Group three	Vegetables, e.g. aubergines, beans, beetroot, broccoli, sprouts, cabbage, carrots, cauliflower, courgettes, parsnips, potatoes, spinach.	Carbohydrates. Minerals especially calcium (green vegetables), potassium, iron (potatoes and green vegetables). Vitamins A (carrots and green leafy vegetables) and C (potatoes and green vegetables). Fibre.
Group four	Meat, fish and eggs.	Protein. Minerals especially calcium (small bones in tinned fish), iron (liver, red meat and egg yolk). Vitamins A, B (complex) and D.
Group five	Dairy foods, i.e. milk, butter, yoghurt, cheese.	Protein, calcium and vitamins A, B (complex) and D.

How much food should baby be eating each day?
Generally, if baby is happy and contented and eating as much as he wants at each meal, then he is probably consuming the right amount of food for him. A satisfactory weight gain is also indicative of an adequate calorie intake. However, for those who are interested in statistics, the approximate average daily calorie requirements of babies aged 0 to two

years are estimated to be as follows:

Age	Calories
0 to three months	515
Three to six months	695
Six to nine months	845
Nine to twelve months	945
Eighteen months	1,150
Two-and-a-half years	1,350

If you calculate all the calories your baby consumes in food and drink each day (the approximate calorific values of all the recipes in this book have been given) you will be able to see how your child compares to the average. If you are seriously concerned that baby may be under- or over-eating, then you should consult your doctor.

When should baby begin feeding himself?
You should start encouraging baby to feed himself when he is about six months old and having his meals in his high-chair.
There are three main ways in which you can do this:

1. By offering finger foods which he can pick up and eat by himself. See Chapter 19 for full instructions on how to prepare them.

2. By helping baby to spoon-feed himself. He may want to take over completely, but as his hand and eye co-ordination is not yet sufficiently developed to enable him to do this with any degree of success, a compromise is required. You can either have a spoon each and you feed him, or share a spoon and let baby feed himself one spoonful for each three you give him. You should decrease your share of the feeding as baby becomes more proficient, so that by twelve to fifteen months baby is spoon-feeding himself most of the time.

3. By letting baby see you and the rest of the family eat, as this will encourage him to copy.

While baby still needs help with his feeding, or if meal-times do not coincide, you could give him his dinner first so that you and the rest of the family can eat in peace, while baby sits in his high-chair with a drink, or toy to play with. Once he is able to feed himself, allowing him to eat at the same time as the rest of the family can be quite successful, providing you are organised. Have baby's dessert, drink, face-cloth, toy etc. all ready to give him as needed, to save you having to interrupt your meal to go and fetch them.

Are there any new problems I am likely to come across once baby is feeding himself?

1. Baby may become a slower eater when left to feed himself, so you will have to allow more time for meals. Don't stand over him with continual offers of assistance. This will not encourage independence. Just give him his food and leave him to get on with it in his own time (no matter how long it takes), while you do something else close-by. He will soon let you know if he needs help, more food, or when he has had enough.

2. Once baby is in control, meal-times may become much messier. Help baby by offering plenty of finger foods and thicker spoon-foods which are less likely to go astray on the hazardous journey from bowl to mouth.

   To make your own job easier, protect baby's clothes with a suitable bib and feed your baby in the kitchen where floors and walls (which may get splashed) are easy to clean.

   Otherwise just ignore the mess until baby has finished his meal completely and clear it all up then. You can console yourself with the fact that things can only get better!

3. You may find that baby likes to dabble with his food as well as eat it. For example, he may decide to abandon his spoon in favour of his fingers or to remove his food from his bowl to his high-chair tray and eat it from there. The novelty value of these experiments will soon wear off so

they are best ignored as long as he is eating as well as playing. When food is smeared around the tray, wiped in his hair or thrown on the floor, etc., complete loss of interest is usually indicated, then remove the offending food at once. Any cries of protest are probably because baby's game has been ruined rather than because he is hungry, but you can try offering the food back *once* if you are unsure!

What should I do if baby won't eat his food?
A baby who won't eat his solid foods when he is relying on them for most or all of his nutritional needs should be treated slightly differently from a baby who rejects them while he is still gaining most of his dietary requirements from milk. Therefore, in addition to following the general advice given in Chapter 2 (as far as it still applies) you should also:

- Try offering a drink, especially if baby may be thirsty or finding food a little dry;

 Offer an alternative, if you think the reason for rejection may be dislike of the original food;

- Offer assistance to a baby who would normally feed himself, but who seems too tired to make the effort (this is about the only time an independent baby will appreciate your interference!).

If none of these suggestions work, you will have to assume that baby is not hungry and end the meal gracefully.

A skipped meal can mean baby will get hungry before he is due to eat again; in this instance a drink or light snack will probably satisfy him until the next meal which could be brought forward a little, if necessary.

If it is the last meal of the day which is not eaten, a filling drink (see Chapter 18) or light supper before bed will stop him going to sleep hungry and possibly waking early for breakfast next morning.

The only time you need worry about your baby not eating occasionally is if he seems off colour (often accompanied by a high temperature). If this happens, he should be watched closely for any developments and the doctor consulted, if necessary.

How can I tell if baby is allergic to something he eats?

The majority of babies are weaned on to a fully mixed diet with no troubles whatsoever. A few may show an allergic reaction to specific foods or to certain types of food.

Food intolerance can manifest itself in many different ways, for example, rashes, diarrhoea, constipation and vomiting. However this list is not exhaustive and the symptoms mentioned can also have many other causes. If you do suspect allergy, withdraw the questionable food temporarily and consult your doctor about what action to take. Never restrict baby's diet permanently without expert advice, otherwise you could be depriving your child of a perfectly nutritious food unnecessarily.

What should I do if baby is choking?

A baby who coughs and splutters while he is eating can still breathe and is not actually choking, but may become frightened. Reassure him gently by talking to him calmly and patting him sharply on the back until he breathes normally.

If baby can't breathe or cough and is panic-stricken then his windpipe is blocked. Tip baby so that his head is lower than his chest. Bang vigorously between his shoulder-blades to try and dislodge the trapped article from his windpipe. If it is coughed up into his mouth, carefully remove the offending article while baby's head is still down, to prevent re-inhalation.

If you are unsuccessful, you should try sitting baby up and looking down his throat. If you can see what is blocking it, try and hook it forward with your finger (do not worry if baby retches, this in itself may create enough pressure to push the trapped object forward). If this doesn't work you will have to rush for help, still holding the baby head downwards.

How should I go about feeding baby away from home?
This depends on where you are going, how you will get there,
what will be available etc. Here are a few tips.

For younger babies
- Take frozen food cubes on a journey to thaw out en route.
  Baby probably won't object to eating food at room
  temperature if used to it.

- Once baby is eating enough, tins and jars of food are very
  useful. Remember to take an opener if using tins!

For older babies
- For babies over six months, buy milk in cartons as needed,
  or carry dried milk powder and mix with tap or bottled
  water for drinking as required.

- Sandwiches can be prepared ready for baby to eat on a
  journey. Or try cheese wedges or hard-boiled eggs with
  bread and butter for a change.

- Fruit can be washed at home and taken on the journey to
  be prepared when required. Remember to take a knife if
  needed!

Generally
- Bottles and cartons of fruit juice for babies can be taken
  and mixed with previously boiled tap, or bottled, water as
  needed. Alternatively, dilute as required at home and carry
  in a flask or baby's bottle. Don't forget to take a special cup
  for baby, if necessary.

- Baby wipes are useful to clean baby's hands and face after
  eating.

- Do not forget bibs, kitchen roll to mop up spills, and towels
  to put over (and possible under) baby's lap to catch crumbs
  (if eating in the car for example). The towel can then be
  shaken out afterwards.

Take as many spoons and bowls as you will need and bags to put them in after use. Alternatively, use disposable paper plates/bowls and spoons which can be thrown away after use. Paper cups are also useful for babies who are able to drink from them.

Spare clothes in case of a catastrophe. These are never needed until you leave them behind!

4. EQUIPMENT

What equipment will I need to prepare baby's food?
This depends on:

- what types of gadgetry you already own;
- the amount of money you want to spend; and
- how much storage/working space you have in your kitchen.

Some devices are almost essential, others just desirable.

1. The electric blender
To me, an electric blender is almost as necessary as a cot or a pram! The initial outlay is high, but you will save money on the amount you would otherwise spend on tins and jars of commercially-prepared baby foods, especially if you have more than one child.

It takes all the hassle out of preparing baby foods. It can:

purée almost any food to a fine or coarse texture in a few seconds;
make delicious frothy drinks; and

- provide a source of fascination to quieten even the hungriest of crying babies. Something which no amount of fork-mashing could ever do!

There are various types of electrically operated blender available. These include:

- family-size blenders;
- hand-held blenders; and
- baby blenders.

FAMILY-SIZE BLENDERS are designed to deal with large portions of food. The minute quantities consumed by babies tend to get stuck below the blades. By the time your child is eating big enough meals to be successfully puréed in a large blender, you will probably be considering chopping most of the food instead.

So big blenders are best reserved for puréeing large quantities of foods suitable for freezing.

Of course, if you already own a food processor (or are thinking of buying one) you will not need to buy a large electric blender as the food processor performs the same functions. You may, however, still want to consider buying a baby blender.

HAND-HELD BLENDERS can be used in any pan or bowl without the need for transferring the food to a special container. However, they may not deal with pieces of stewed meat, for example, as successfully as goblet-type liquidisers and this should be borne in mind if you intend to buy one.

BABY BLENDERS are the most suitable for liquidising baby foods. They can deal equally well with very small quantities of food or with bigger amounts for freezing. (Although the capacity of a big blender is larger, baby won't want the same purée repeatedly for weeks. There is also a limit to freezer storage time and space.)

An ideal blender should:

- blend at one easily controllable speed, making it easy to achieve a fine or coarse texture;
- be so small it can be stored with your crockery;
- be dismantled easily for cleaning; and
- allow extra liquid to be added through a hole in the lid.

It is also possible to buy MANUALLY OPERATED BLENDERS. They usually cope well with cooked vegetables, struggle with fish and find meat almost impossible. Do not invest in one if you already own a sieve and a fork!

2. The sieve
A metal or plastic sieve with a fairly fine mesh is vital for removing skins and pips from fruit and vegetables for very young babies. It is also good for straining finely chopped food which may fall through the holes of a colander. Buy the best quality you can afford but be prepared to replace it quite often (a few months of pushing food through one with the back of a spoon will soon force holes in it). All sieves are difficult to clean. Plastic sieves have the advantage of being able to be sterilised using a chemical method. The bowl of some metal sieves can be removed and sterilised by immersing in boiling water for a few minutes.

3. Strainer
The use of a small strainer when preparing baby drinks from fresh citrus fruits, for example, will prevent the clogging of teats and holes in the tops of bottles and trainer cups with any tiny particles of pulp.

4. Cheese grater
A grater can perform some of the functions of a blender and is easier to clean. It is especially useful for grating cheese, fruit and vegetables. Essential if you do not own a blender.

5. Small saucepan with lid
Preferably non-stick and heavy-based. Necessary for simmering small quantities of food with minimal liquid and as little loss of steam and nutrients as possible.

6. Small milk pan
Preferably non-stick and heavy-based. Necessary for making baby-sized meals and sauces etc.

7. Ramekin
Good for baking, steaming, putting under the grill and in pressure cookers. Can also be used for serving food.

8. Small individual pie dishes
As above, but for slightly larger portions.

9. Small casserole with lid
Half-pint capacity. The type which can be used on the hob and in the oven is preferable. Good for making baby-sized casseroles and stews etc. which are too large for pie dishes or ramekins, but which would get lost in larger vessels.

10. Measuring jug, spoons, scales, etc.
Some people manage without them, but they are essential if guess-work is not one of your strong points!

11. Pressure cooker
By no means essential, but useful for cooking some foods quickly, e.g. pulses, and several foods all at once. If you have one, take advantage of it. See recipes for pressure cookers in Part III.

12. Double saucepan
Not vital, but good for making custards. However, a bowl in a saucepan of simmering water will suffice.

13. Containers for storage
Small bowls, covered by saucers or foil, for example, are adequate for home use. Small plastic tubs and boxes are good for travelling as they are virtually indestructible. Do not use them for strong-smelling foods though as they tend to retain odours. Glass is better in this respect.

14. *Miscellaneous*
Aluminium foil is good for covering food, cooking food in its own juices in the oven, and for covering ramekins and pie dishes, etc.

A *fork* is needed to mash soft foods, which do not need to be blended, such as potatoes and bananas.

A *stiff brush* is useful for cleaning vegetables, e.g. potatoes and carrots for cooking in their skins.

A *sharp knife* is required for slicing, chopping, dicing, etc.

A *potato peeler* for peeling fruit and vegetables thinly.

A *juice squeezer* for extracting juice from citrus fruits.

A *spatula* for use with an electric blender to move food from the side into the blade area.

What feeding equipment do I need to buy?
1. *High-chair*
When you first start to feed baby he may be quite happy on your lap or in a baby-chair. By the age of five to six months he will become restless reclining, and try to sit upright. This is the time to transfer him to a high-chair. When choosing a high-chair pick one with:

- a wide base for stability;
- an adjustable, removable easy-to-clean tray with raised edge to catch spills; and
  an easy-to-clean (non-fabric) seat.

Alternatively, buy a seat that fastens to the edge of a table or worktop. This is cheaper and takes up less space.

2. *Dishes*
Two plastic/unbreakable baby dishes are all you need. Compartments that can be filled with hot water to keep food warm are unnecessary - you will probably find that cooling food is your biggest problem! Plates with sections are no more essential for a baby than an adult. China dishes look very pretty, but are easily broken (even the most well-behaved baby will drop his plate on the floor occasionally to

let you know he has finished!). Suction caps, however, *are* useful. They help to keep the bowl still while baby is learning to feed himself and stop it being thrown on the floor or used as a hat!

3. Spoons and forks

You will need a very small spoon at first, and later, spoons with wider and deeper bowls. Plastic spoons are best because they are soft on the gums and light to handle. Plastic forks are not very useful (they are more likely to split soft food than pierce it for picking up), but as they are generally sold in packs with the spoons you will end up with a few anyway.

4. Bibs

Large bibs are necessary. Many people find pelican bibs very good, once baby can sit up straight. I have always found that the absorbent towelling waterproof-backed bibs with sleeves protect baby's clothes very well, providing you can get the tray of the high-chair close enough to the baby to stop food going on to his lap. If you can't, a towel round his waist should do the trick.

Smaller bibs are adequate for drinks and teething dribbles.

Avoid flat plastic bibs which allow food to run straight off on to baby.

5. Cups

Some have no handles, some one, some two. Which type you choose is a matter of (baby's) personal preference. Some are weighted so they are less likely to fall over when put down awkwardly. These are rather heavy for young babies to use, and more experienced drinkers wouldn't need them. The sizes of cups and holes in trainer tops vary. A little cup with small holes is best at first; gradually baby will progress to using larger cups and bigger holes. Clear cups allow you to see what you are doing when mixing drinks and the quantity baby has drunk.

6. Face-cloths

You will need a supply of face-cloths which can be moistened with warm water to clean baby's face, hands, hair, ears, or whatever! This is preferable to smearing chemicals, in the form of baby wipes, over baby's face and hands, or to smearing washing-up liquid over him because you are using the dish-cloth.

7. Mat on the floor

If you can feed baby on a floor that can be wiped clean (for example, kitchen tiles or lino), a mat or newspaper underneath the high-chair are unnecessary. It is just as easy to wipe spills off the floor as it is to clean a mat or pick up newspaper – you would have to remove the food that missed the mat or newspaper anyway!

5. FOOD HANDLING AND STORAGE

What are the basic principles of safe food handling?
The five basic principles are:

1. Always work with clean hands and handle foods no more than necessary.

2. Make sure all utensils and work-surfaces are clean and dry.

3. Prepare food as quickly as possible after removal from the refrigerator.

4. Cooked food, if not to be served immediately, should be covered, cooled quickly, and refrigerated or frozen.

5. If reheating food for baby, bring gently up to boiling point, and allow to cool to required temperature before serving. Throw away any left-overs that are not eaten.

What, how and how long should foods be stored in a pantry?
All storage times given below are approximate depending
on:-

1. Pantry/store-cupboard conditions
- The pantry or store-cupboard should be as cool as possible
  (the ideal temperature is about 50°F/10°C). It should be
  located on an outside wall, or on a cold north/north-east
  facing wall to avoid prolonged contact with direct sunlight;
  away from sources of heat, e.g. the oven, radiators and
  refrigerator exhaust, etc.

- It should be as dry and dark as possible. The door(s) should
  be kept shut to keep out light and steam.

  The pantry should be ventilated to keep the air fresh. The
  window or ventilator should be covered by gauze to keep
  insects away.

- Walls, floors and shelves should be smooth, in good repair
  with a washable surface for regular easy cleaning and light
  in colour for good illumination.

- Shelving should also be shallow and easily reachable for
  safe, trouble-free storage.

2. The age and quality of food when bought
- Food should be as fresh as possible. Check the 'best by
  date' regularly and consume older food first.

Food	How to store	How long to store for
Cereals Wholegrain cereals including rice, barley, oatmeal, rye, wheat, and wheatgerm.	In unopened original packs or in airtight containers after opening.	3 – 6 months or until 'best by date' on pack.

Food	How to store	How long to store for
Wholemeal flour.	As above.	1 month or until 'best by date' on pack.
Wholewheat pasta (all types).	As above.	6 months or until 'best by date' on pack.
Breakfast cereals.	As above.	1 month or until 'best by date' on pack.
Bread.	In wrapper (or clean polythene bag for uncut loaves) in ventilated bin. The end of the bag should be loosely folded under the loaf to allow air to circulate.	Varies with type of bread. Usually 3 – 4 days. Crisp bread and rolls should be consumed on day of purchase.

Fruit

Apricots, apples, avocado pears, cherries, kiwi fruit, mangoes, nectarines, peaches, dessert pears, plums.	At room temperature.	Until ripe and then eaten or refrigerated for a few days.
Bananas.	As above.	Until ripe and then eaten. (Never refrigerate as they go black.)

Food	How to store	How long to store for
Melon, pineapples.	As above.	Until ripe. (Never refrigerate unless well-wrapped as they can impart flavour to other foods especially milk and butter.)
Tinned fruit.	Unopened.	1 year.
Dried fruit.	In unopened original pack or in an airtight container after opening.	3 months or until 'best by date' on pack.
Tomatoes.	In a paper bag or in a drawer at room temperature to ripen.	Until ripe when they should be consumed or refrigerated for a few days.

Vegetables

Food	How to store	How long to store for
Potatoes, sweet potatoes, onions, winter squash, swede, beetroot, turnips.	Unwashed in a vegetable rack in a dark, airy and cool place if possible.	A week or so at room temperature. Up to 2 – 3 months at 50 – 55°F (10 – 13°C).
Leeks.	As above.	Up to 3 days at room temperature. A little longer at 50 – 55°F (10 – 13°C).
Tinned vegetables.	Unopened.	1 year.

Food	How to store	How long to store for
Dried vegetables including lentils, peas and beans.	In unopened original packs or in an airtight container after opening.	1 year.
Meat		
Tinned meat except ham over 2 lb (900g).	Unopened.	1 year.
(Ham over 2 lb (900g) should be refrigerated and used within 6 months).		
Fish		
Tinned fish.	Unopened.	1 year.
Eggs	Pointed end down, away from strong-smelling foods as the shells are porous.	7 – 10 days at 50 – 55°F (10 – 13°C). Less if temperature is higher.
Butter	In covered dish.	Up to 1 week while in use.
Miscellaneous		
Honey, essences, gelatine, cocoa/ carob powder,	In original containers, except boxed cocoa/carob	1 year.

Food	How to store	How long to store for
Marmite, tomato purée, oils.	powder which should be transferred to a dry airtight container after opening.	
Herbs, spices and seasonings.	In airtight containers in a dark place (e.g. in rack on inside of cupboard/ pantry door).	6 months.
Baking powder.	In original or airtight and dry container.	3 months or until 'best by date' on pack.
Dried milk powder.	In original container.	3 months.
Unrefined sugar.	In unopened original pack or in a dry airtight container after opening.	1 month.
Nuts.	As above.	1 month.

What, how and how long should foods be stored in a refrigerator?
Refrigeration prolongs the storage life of perishable foods by reducing the activity of micro organisms and enzymes which cause deterioration. All storage times given below are approximate depending on –

1. Refrigeration conditions
The temperature of the refrigerator should be between 35

45°F (1.6 – 7°C). Generally, the coldest part is nearest the frozen food compartment, the warmest at the bottom. Thermometers are available to hang in a refrigerator, enabling you to see at a glance whether a lower setting is needed in warmer weather, or when the fridge is full, etc.

Foods should be stored in their correct places to make best use of low temperatures. For example:

– meat, poultry, fish, cheese and yoghurt should be stored in the coldest part (usually under the frozen food compartment);

– cooked meats and made-up dishes on the middle shelves;

fruit and vegetables in the bottom (including the salad/crisper drawer); and

– butter, eggs and milk in the door.

It is important not to pack foods too closely, so as to allow free circulation of air. Loose coverings or wrappings are also essential to prevent dryness and odour contamination.

The door should be opened as little as possible and very hot foods cooled before refrigerating to prevent the temperature inside being raised too much, which wastes fuel and causes excessive frosting.

Regular defrosting is necessary to enable the refrigerator to run efficiently. Cleaning can be done with a weak solution of bicarbonate of soda, which removes stains, but does not impart an odour of its own. All surfaces must be dried well before putting food back into the cabinet.

2. The age and quality of food when bought
- Only fresh foods should be stored in the refrigerator. Check the 'best by date' regularly and consume older food first.

Food	How to store	How long to store for
Fruit		
Apricots, avocado pears, cherries, kiwi fruit, mangoes, nectarines, peaches, dessert pears, plums.	Loosely wrapped in a polythene bag in the warmest part of the refrigerator.	When ripe for a few days.
Grapefruits, oranges, lemons, limes, apples (when ripe).	As above.	Up to 2 weeks.
Tomatoes (when ripe).	As above.	Up to 2 weeks.
Vegetables		
Asparagus, broccoli, sprouts, spinach, corn, greens, lettuce (other than iceberg lettuces), mushrooms, peas.	As above.	2 – 3 days.
Aubergines, green beans, carrots, cauliflowers, celery, courgettes, cucumbers, iceberg lettuces, parsnips, peppers.	As above.	Up to 1 week.
Cabbages.	As above.	Up to 2 weeks.

Food	How to store	How long to store for
Raw Meat Meat and poultry.	Clean quickly under running cold water, pat dry with paper kitchen towel and cover loosely with polythene or foil.	2 – 5 days or as directed on label if pre-packed.
Minced meat and offal.	Covered loosely in a non-airtight container. (Rinse and pat offal quickly before use.)	1 – 2 days or as directed on label if pre-packed.
Raw Fish	Clean quickly under running cold water, pat dry with paper kitchen towel and cover loosely with polythene or foil.	1 day or as directed on label if pre-packed.
Eggs	Pointed end down, away from strong-smelling foods, in door.	Up to 2 weeks.
Raw egg yolks.	Covered with water if whole.	2 days.
Raw egg whites.	In a covered container or dish.	2 days.

Food	How to store	How long to store for
Dairy foods		
Milk.	In original bottle, unopened until required.	Up to 4 days.
Yoghurt.	In original container.	As directed on carton.
Butter.	In original pack until required.	2 – 4 weeks or until 'best by date' on pack.
Soft cheeses.	In original pack or tightly wrapped in polythene or foil.	About a week or until 'best by date' on pack.
Hard cheese.	As above.	About 2 weeks or until 'best by date' on pack.
Cottage cheese.	In original carton.	As directed on carton.
Cooked or prepared foods		
Cereal purées.	In a covered container or dish.	1 day.
Raw fruit purées.	As above.	As above.
Cooked fruit purées.	As above.	As above.
Vegetable dishes and purées.	As above.	As above.

Food	How to store	How long to store for
Cooked meats.	Loosely covered with polythene or foil.	2 days.
Meat dishes and purées.	In a covered container or dish.	1 day.
Cooked fish.	Loosely covered with polythene or foil.	As above.
Fish dishes and purées.	In a covered container or dish.	1 day.
Boiled egg still in its shell.	Uncovered.	Up to 1 week.
Soups and other combination dishes.	In a covered container or dish.	1 day.
Desserts.	As above.	As above.
Home-made beverages.	In an airtight container.	As above.
Commercially-prepared fruit juices.	In original container or as directed thereon.	As directed on original container.
Opened tinned foods.	In a covered container or dish.	1 day.

What, how and how long should foods be stored in a freezer?
Food can be preserved for long periods in a freezer because
enzyme activity and the growth of micro organisms are
rendered almost inactive below 0°F (-18°C).

Foods may be stored for the times given below, provided –

1. Only top quality food is frozen.
2. Freezing takes place without delay.
3. Cooked foods are brought down to room temperature or
   lower before freezing.
4. Foods are correctly wrapped, excluding as much air as
   possible.

In addition –
Foods should be suitably labelled with content, quantity
and date of freezing.

Check 'best by dates' regularly and consume older food
first.

It is not safe to re-freeze food which has already been
frozen and thawed, although you may re-freeze food which
has been previously frozen, provided it is cooked first.

Foods stored for longer than the times recommended
below may show a deterioration in texture and flavour,
although they may still be safe to eat.

Food	How to store	How long to store for
Fruit Most fruits with the exception of strawberries and pears.	Suitably prepared and packed.	Up to 12 months.
Vegetables Most vegetables with the exception of salad vegetables.	Suitably prepared and packed.	Up to 12 months.

Food	How to store	How long to store for
Meat		
Beef, lamb and chicken	Wrapped tightly in moisture/vapour-proof wrappings to exclude air.	9 – 12 months.
Minced meat and offal	As above.	3 months.
Fish	As above.	6 months.
Eggs		
Egg whites and yolks (separately).	In airtight containers.	9 – 12 months.

Cooked or prepared foods
The following can be stored up to 1 month as detailed below: cereal purées; fruit purées; vegetable dishes and purées; meat dishes and purées; fish dishes and purées; soups and other combination dishes; and desserts.

What are the best ways to freeze food for baby?
Fresh meat, fish and poultry can be bought half to one pound (225g to 450g) at a time, divided into two ounce (50g) portions, tightly wrapped in foil and frozen for the storage times given above. The night before they are needed, they can be taken out of the freezer and allowed to thaw overnight in the refrigerator before being used in any of the recipes in Part III of this book.

Suitable recipes from Parts II and III can also be made in larger quantities than required and frozen in single portions which can be thawed and reheated (if necessary) as needed. To do this:

a) When dealing with very small quantities for younger babies
1. Prepare or cook food as appropriate, purée, cover and refrigerate (if cooked) until cold. Uncooked food which

has been puréed with an electric blender should also be covered and refrigerated to allow the contents to settle.

2. Pour food into icecube trays (allowing a little room for expansion).

3. Freeze cubes.

4. If the trays are needed, turn out the cubes and wrap them tightly in foil. Pack in plastic freezer bags secured with tie twists, or suitable-sized airtight containers.

5. Label bags/containers with date, contents and quantity.

b) When dealing with larger quantities for older babies
1. Prepare or cook food as appropriate. Purée, mash or chop as necessary (or leave until food is to be served), cover and refrigerate (if cooked) until cold. Uncooked food which has been puréed with an electric blender should also be covered and refrigerated to allow the contents to settle.

2. If food has been cooked in single-size portions in freezer-proof containers, providing there is a little room for expansion, tightly cover with foil and freeze as it is. (Small foil containers are available which can be used for cooking, freezing and reheating, without tying up your supply of dishes.)
    If food has been prepared in one large batch, transfer to single-portion-sized foil or plastic containers, allowing a little room for expansion once again, and cover with foil, or lids.

3. Freeze.

4. If the containers are needed, turn out the blocks of frozen food (by dipping in boiling water first, if necessary) and wrap tightly in foil. Pack in plastic freezer bags secured with tie twists, or suitable-sized containers.

5. Label bags/containers with date, contents and quantity.

What are the best ways to thaw and reheat baby's food?
If baby doesn't mind, you may thaw any previously cooked and frozen dish (either overnight in the fridge or at room temperature for as short a time as necessary) and serve without reheating. Aim to do this with foods that are usually eaten cold such as fruit purées and desserts.

Food may be reheated from frozen or after it has been allowed to thaw out as above. Either:

– put food straight into a suitable-sized saucepan with a little milk, water or stock as appropriate and bring gently to the boil, stirring often to prevent sticking; or

– wrap in foil or put into a lidded casserole and place in a preheated oven, gas mark 6 (400°F/200°C), for twenty minutes, or until food appears as hot when reheated as if it has just been cooked.

Can I use a microwave oven to thaw and reheat baby's food?
Previously cooked and frozen food may be thawed and reheated in a microwave oven provided care is taken to ensure that the food is *thoroughly* reheated so that *all* of the food is as hot when reheated as if it has just been cooked.

Eggs
Since this book was first published, much concern has been expressed about the possibility of eggs being contaminated with salmonella. You should consult your doctor, or health visitor, or the Department of Health, since there is a view that small children are a vulnerable group who should not eat raw or lightly cooked eggs.

If you want thoroughly cooked eggs, then adapt my recipes which contain raw or lightly cooked eggs as follows: cook the egg until both white and yolk are firm, then mash or blend it with a little milk or water, as necessary, to achieve the desired consistency, before following the rest of the recipe.

6. GETTING ORGANISED

In what ways can I plan ahead when preparing baby's food?
1. By making sure you have all the ingredients you will need in stock before you begin to prepare any freshly cooked food for baby.

2. By making sure your supply of frozen meals is sufficient if relying on them to feed baby.

3. By keeping some commercially-prepared baby foods ready for emergencies such as:

   – when another person suddenly has to give baby his food because you can't be there;

   – when you have accidentally run out of cubes, or do not have all the ingredients you thought you did have;

   – when baby does not like what you have prepared, is still hungry, and you do not have a readily available alternative. This applies especially to babies, who have not been introduced to a wide range of foods.

4. By having some 'healthy' instant snacks on hand to act as a 'patience-preserver' for times when baby is screaming with hunger and his meal is not quite ready. You can try any of the following on babies who are over six months, but see Chapter 19 for more finger food ideas:

   - low-sugar rusks;
   - dry crackers;
   - crisp-type snacks;
   - pieces of dry instant breakfast cereal such as Allinson's Crunchy Bran;
   - little squares of bread and butter/Marmite;
   - thin slices or tiny cubes of cheese; and
   - slices of banana.

Do not offer too much or you will spoil baby's appetite for his meal. Dry foods can be soaked in milk first, if necessary, to soften them a little. If you intend to give baby crackers, crisps, cereal and the like, buy those varieties containing the least artificial additives, salt and sugar, etc. It is not advisable to let baby see that you have more of your chosen patience-preserver than what you have given him, or he may decide he would prefer that to the meal you have lovingly prepared for him!

How can I save time and money?
1. You need not always prepare meals especially for baby, you can also let him eat what the rest of the family is having, provided;

   - a suitable method of cooking is used;

   - baby's portion is removed before the addition of any salt and (for babies under six months) spices;

   - sweet dishes have been prepared without the addition of any sugar, or with a minimal amount of unrefined sugar, or honey, where necessary.

Simply purée, mash or chop baby's portion and let him have his:

- with the rest of the family if convenient;

- on his own beforehand; or

- later on or the next day, if food is covered, cooled quickly and refrigerated etc.

You could also make a larger amount for the family than required so that some could be frozen in baby meal-size portions to be given within the next month or so.

2. If using the oven for the rest of the family, put a little something in for baby at the same time to conserve energy. For example, try cooking almost any raw food wrapped in lightly buttered aluminium foil in a moderate oven until tender. There is nothing to clean up; simply throw away the foil after use.

3. Cook baby's food in the same pots and pans either immediately before, during or after preparing the family's food to save washing-up.

4. If freezing, cook several fruits, vegetables etc., together in the same saucepan then purée in combinations or individually as required.

5. If using the blender to purée different foods, simply rinse out between each type and wash at the end.

6. Pressure cookers are useful if you need to prepare a meal in a hurry. See recipes using pressure cookers in Part III.

How do I use and modify the recipes in this book?
All spoon measurements are level unless otherwise stated.
Throughout the recipes the term 'electric blender' means any type of electric blender unless otherwise stated. 'Hand

blender' refers to manually operated (non-electric) blenders.

Full instructions on how to prepare fruit, vegetables, meat and fish for cooking or eating raw are given in Parts II and III.

No quantities have been given for the recipes for the purées, so you can decide how much you wish to make at any one time.

In Part III, apart from Chapter 8, the quantities given are, generally, the smallest practical for one baby, but they may still be too much for very small babies. To avoid too much food wastage, remove what you think baby will eat and;

- refrigerate or freeze the rest for another meal;
- have the rest for your lunch; or
- add to suitable family dishes.

Similar action can also be taken to save throwing away the partly-used eggs and pieces of fruit and vegetables, etc., which are needed in some of the recipes.

Left-over stocks which you may decide to pour off instead of boil down can be used very successfully in family soups, stews, casseroles, etc. or simply as a nutritious drink for yourself or baby!

Where larger quantities than those given in the recipe are required, for example, for: older babies; more than one baby; you and baby; or freezing in bulk; simply double, treble, etc., everything in the recipe and proceed as normal.

Can I substitute one ingredient for another similar ingredient if I want to?

When you have been using these recipes for a while, you will probably find many ways of altering them slightly to suit your own baby's particular tastes. Below are some substitutions which I have made while preparing this book:

1. Where a recipe calls for tomato juice you may use:

   - fresh tomatoes, puréed as in Chapter 7 (one medium tomato yields about two tablespoons);

- freshly opened tomato juice out of a carton or tin; or
- sieved Italian plum tomatoes.

2. Most of the recipes have been thickened with wheatgerm because it is nutritious and has a bland flavour making it suitable for use in sweet and savoury dishes. If baby does not like wheatgerm you may use:

   - baby rice, but this will whiten and impart a very ricy flavour, or
   - cornflour (mixed to a smooth paste with an equal quantity of cold water), but this has little or no nutritive value.

3. Fruit tinned in fruit juice e.g. apricots, peaches, pears and pineapple may be drained well and used instead of fresh fruit in any of the recipes in this book.

4. Frozen, tinned or fresh vegetables are all suitable for baby and may be substituted as appropriate in any of the recipes in this book. Cooking times may vary though. So where, for example, a recipe calls for frozen peas, you may use: tinned peas, which are already cooked and only require draining and reheating; or fresh peas, provided you extend the cooking time, if necessary.

   When buying tinned vegetables, always choose those varieties which contain the minimum of unnecessary additives (e.g. salt, sugar, colouring and flavouring).

PART TWO

RECIPES FOR BEGINNERS

(from around 4 months)

7. CEREAL, FRUIT AND VEGETABLE PURÉES

All the purées may be stored in a refrigerator for up to 24 hours, or frozen for up to a month, unless specified otherwise in the recipes.

CEREALS
Nutrient content: Cereals are a good source of carbohydrate, incomplete protein, minerals, B vitamins and vitamin E.
Availability: Some wholegrain cereals are available from supermarkets. All are available in good healthfood shops.
To buy: Always buy from a reputable dealer to ensure you get the freshest cereals possible. Pre-packed cereals usually carry a 'best by date', which is a good guide to their age and potential storage life.
To store: Cereals should be stored in a cool, dry atmosphere – they should never be exposed to steam which causes rapid deterioration in quality. They are best transferred to an airtight container after opening. Always wash and thoroughly dry containers before filling with cereal – never mix an old batch of cereal with a new one.

CEREAL PURÉE (Using wholegrain rice flakes, barleyflakes, oatflakes, ryeflakes or wheatflakes.)

Calories: 100 (approx.) per 1 oz/25g raw weight
Cooking time: up to 20 minutes

Put the required amount of flakes into a small saucepan. For each spoonful or cupful of flakes add 3 spoonfuls or cupfuls of water respectively. Bring just up to boiling point, lower the heat, cover and simmer very gently until all the liquid is absorbed.

Purée with an electric/hand blender or push through a sieve with the back of a spoon to get a smoother texture, if necessary. Add a little previously boiled water if a thinner consistency is required.

Cereal purée can also be made using commercially-prepared baby cereals. These are refined cereals which are made more nutritious by being fortified with vitamins and minerals. Follow the manufacturer's directions for age at which to start and how to prepare.

There is no need to store these purées which can be made very quickly in small quantities as and when required.

FRUIT PURÉES

APPLE
Nutrient content: Apples contain carbohydrate, minerals especially potassium, some of the B vitamins and vitamins C and E.
To buy: Look for firm, brightly coloured fruit with unblemished skins.
To store: Apples are best stored at room temperature until ripe and then eaten, or loosely wrapped in a polythene bag and transferred to the warmest part of the refrigerator, where they will keep for up to two weeks.
To prepare: Wash, quarter, core and peel apple.

RAW APPLE PURÉE (Using any dessert apple of your choice.)
No cooking　　　　　*Calories: 50 (approx.) per apple*
Purée the required amount of prepared apple to a smooth

texture with an electric blender (this makes the finest purée), or grate, using the finest section of a cheese grater. Add a little previously boiled water if a thinner consistency is required.
To store: This purée should be served straightaway.

COOKED APPLE PURÉE (Using any cooking apple of your choice.)
Calories: 10 (approx.) per 1 oz/25g raw weight
Cooking time: about 10 minutes
Slice the required amount of prepared apple and place in a suitable-sized saucepan (there is no need to add water). Cook over a moderate heat, stirring all the time to prevent sticking, until the apple is soft and mushy. Sweeten to taste with a little unrefined sugar while the apple is still hot (the heat should melt the sugar). Purée to a smooth texture using an electric/hand blender, push through a sieve with the back of a spoon, or mash finely with a fork, adding a little previously boiled water to thin down a little if necessary.

APRICOT
Nutrient content: Apricots contain carbohydrate, minerals especially potassium, vitamin A, some of the B vitamins and a little of vitamins C and E.
To buy: Choose apricots with smooth, velvety skins which are free from blemishes. Under-ripe fruit are hard and sour; ripe fruit yield gently to pressure and have a milder flavour.
To store: Store as for Apple, page 70. Ripe ones will keep for a few days.
To prepare: No special preparation necessary.

RAW APRICOT PURÉE
No cooking   *Calories: 8 (approx.) per apricot*
Cover the required amount of apricots for about 30 seconds with water that has just boiled to loosen skins, then gently peel with your fingers. Cut the flesh in segments away from the stone and purée to a smooth texture using an electric/hand blender or mash finely with a fork.

COOKED APRICOT PURÉE (Using fresh apricots.)
Cooking time: 10 minutes
Place the required amount of apricots in a suitable-sized saucepan with just enough water to cover. Bring to the boil, lower the heat, cover with a fitting lid and simmer for 10 minutes or until tender. Drain. Purée to a smooth texture by pushing through a sieve with the back of a spoon, discarding skins and stones, or peel and mash the flesh finely with a fork.

You can also prepare cooked apricot purée using moisturised and ready-to-eat dried apricots available from supermarkets. Follow the instructions for prune purée on page 80.

AUBERGINE
Nutrient content: Aubergines contain a little incomplete protein and carbohydrate, minerals especially potassium, some of the B vitamins and vitamin C.
To buy: Look for well-formed aubergines with smooth, shiny, dark, unblemished skins.
To store: Aubergines are best stored loosely wrapped in a polythene bag in the warmest part of the refrigerator where they will keep for up to a week.
To prepare: Wash quickly in running cold water and dry with paper kitchen towel.

AUBERGINE PURÉE
                    Calories: 30 (approx.) per aubergine
Cooking time: 10 minutes
Cut the required amount of prepared aubergine into fairly large chunks and place in a suitable-sized saucepan with enough cold water to come halfway up the sides. Bring to the boil, lower the heat, cover with a fitting lid and simmer for 10 minutes or until tender. Drain through a sieve. Purée to a smooth texture using an electric/hand blender, or by pushing through a sieve with the back of a spoon.

AVOCADO
Nutrient content: Avocado pears contain a little incomplete protein, a fair amount of fat, a little carbohydrate, minerals

especially potassium, vitamin A, some of the B vitamins, and vitamins C and E.

To buy: Look for well-formed fruits with shiny unblemished skins. They are ripe to eat when they yield all over to gentle pressure.

To store: Store as for Apple, page 70. Ripe ones will keep for a few days.

To prepare: Wash, slice in half, remove stone and scoop out required amount of flesh with a spoon. Any unused avocado should be sprinkled with lemon juice, covered tightly with polythene or foil and eaten as soon as possible.

AVOCADO PURÉE

No cooking   *Calories: 450 (approx.) per pear*

Mash the flesh finely with a fork, adding as much previously boiled water as necessary to get a purée of the right consistency.

To store: This purée should be served straightaway.

BANANA

Nutrient content: Bananas contain carbohydrate, minerals especially potassium, vitamin A, a little of the B vitamins and vitamins C and E.

To buy: Choose slightly under-ripe bananas with smooth unbruised skins and ripen at home. Bananas are ready to eat when they have brown spots on their skins.

To store: Bananas should be stored at room temperature and eaten when ripe.

To prepare: Slice off only as much banana as you intend to use, then peel. (Any left-over unpeeled banana will keep for about a day.)

BANANA PURÉE

No cooking   *Calories: 60 (approx.) per small banana*

Mash the required amount of prepared banana very finely with a fork, adding as much previously boiled water as necessary to achieve the desired consistency.

To store: Banana purée should be made as required and eaten straightaway.

BERRY AND CURRANT (Including bilberries, blackberries, blackcurrants, cranberries, gooseberries, loganberries, mulberries, raspberries, redcurrants and strawberries.)
Nutrient content: Berries and currants contain carbohydrates, minerals especially potassium, vitamin A, some of the
B vitamins, vitamin C and a little vitamin E.
Availability: Different varieties are available during summer
and autumn.
To buy: Look for plump, fresh, evenly coloured fruit with no
signs of leaking or mould.
To store: Store unwashed, loosely covered in a polythene bag
in the warmest part of the refrigerator, where they will keep
for up to 3 days.
To prepare: Wash quickly in a sieve or colander under
running cold water and remove any stalks, leaves and
damaged fruit etc. Watch carefully for grubs in raspberries
and loganberries.

COOKED BERRY/CURRANT PURÉE
               Calories: 8 (approx.) per 1 oz/25g raw weight
Cooking time: 10 – 15 minutes
Put the required amount of prepared fruit into a suitable-
sized saucepan with a little water, if necessary. Bring up to
simmering point, cover with a fitting lid and continue to
simmer for 10 minutes, or until the fruit is soft and mushy.
Sweeten to taste with a little unrefined sugar if needed, while
the fruit is still hot (the heat should melt the sugar). Purée to a
smooth texture by pushing through a sieve with the back of a
spoon, discarding the skin and seeds.

RAW BERRY PURÉE (Using strawberries or raspberries.)
No cooking   *Calories: 8 (approx.) per 1 oz/25g*
Purée the required amount of prepared fruit to a smooth
texture by pushing through a sieve with the back of a spoon,
discarding the seeds.

CHERRY
Nutrient content: Cherries contain carbohydrates, minerals

especially potassium, vitamin A, some of the B vitamins and vitamin C.

Availability: Cherries are available in the summer.

To buy: Buy firm cherries with shiny skins, avoiding any discoloured or shrivelled fruit.

To store: Store as for Apple, page 70. Ripe ones will keep for a few days.

To prepare: Remove stems and wash quickly in a colander or sieve under running cold water.

CHERRY PURÉE

Calories: 12 (approx.) per 1 oz/25g raw weight
Cooking time: about 10 minutes

Put the required amount of cherries into a suitable-sized saucepan with just enough water to moisten the bottom of the pan. Bring to simmering point, cover with a fitting lid and continue to simmer for 10 minutes or until the cherries are soft and mushy. Sweeten to taste if necessary with a little unrefined sugar while still hot. Remove the stones and purée to a smooth texture using an electric/hand blender.

FIG

Nutrient content: Figs contain carbohydrate, minerals especially potassium, vitamin A and some of the B vitamins.

Availability: Moisturised and ready-to-eat dried figs are available from supermarkets.

To buy: Look for longest 'best by date' on pack.

To store: Follow instructions on pack.

To prepare: Wash in a colander or sieve under running cold water.

FIG PURÉE

Calories: 50 (approx.) per 1 oz/25g dry weight
Cooking time: 15 – 20 minutes

Place the required amount of figs in a suitable-sized saucepan with just enough cold water to cover. Bring to the boil, lower the heat, cover with a fitting lid and simmer for about 15 minutes, or until the fruit is plump and tender. Drain the figs through a sieve, reserving the cooking liquid. Purée to a smooth texture by pushing through a sieve with the back of a spoon, discarding the seeds and adding as much of the cooking liquid as necessary to achieve the desired consistency.

GRAPE

Nutrient content: Grapes contain carbohydrate, minerals especially potassium, some of the B vitamins and a little vitamin C.

To buy: Look for well-coloured firm grapes which are firmly attached to the stems.

To store: Store unwashed, loosely covered in a polythene bag in the warmest part of the refrigerator, where they will keep for a few days.

To prepare: Wash quickly in a colander or sieve under running cold water.

GRAPE PURÉE
No cooking   *Calories: 15 (approx.) per 1 oz/25g*
Cut the required amount of grapes in half and purée to a smooth texture by pushing through a sieve with the back of a spoon, discarding the skins and seeds.

GRAPEFRUIT & ORANGE

Nutrient content: Grapefruits and oranges contain carbohydrate, minerals especially potassium, some of the B vitamins and vitamin C.

To buy: Choose fruit which is firm, well-shaped and heavy in comparison with its size.

To store: Store loosely covered in a polythene bag in the warmest part of the refrigerator for up to 2 weeks.

To prepare: Wash, peel (removing as much pith as possible), divide into segments and take out the pips.

GRAPEFRUIT/ORANGE PURÉE
No cooking   *Calories: 35 (approx.) per small whole fruit*
Put the required amount of prepared fruit into an electric blender and purée to a smooth texture. Add a little honey to grapefruit purée and blend again if baby finds it too tart.

MANGO
Nutrient content: Mangoes contain carbohydrate, some minerals especially potassium, vitamins A and C and some of the B vitamins.

To buy: Choose mangoes with smooth unblemished skins. When they are ripe they will yield slightly to gentle pressure.

To store: Store as for Apple, page 70. Ripe ones will keep for a few days.

To prepare: Wash first, then using a sharp knife, cut a thick lengthways slice from each side of the fruit as close to the stone as possible. Scoop out the flesh with a spoon, then peel the centre section and carefully cut the rest of the flesh away from the stone.

MANGO PURÉE

No cooking   *Calories: 80 (approx.) per mango*

Purée the required amount of mango to a smooth texture using an electric/hand blender.

MELON
Nutrient content: Melons contain carbohydrate, minerals especially potassium, vitamin A, some of the B vitamins and vitamin C.

To buy: A ripe melon should have a pleasant odour and yield to gentle pressure on the end opposite the stem end.

To store: Melons should be stored at room temperature until ripe and then eaten.

To prepare: Wash first then cut into wedges, scoop out the seeds and cut away the peel with a sharp knife. (Any unused wedges should be wrapped tightly in polythene or foil, stored in the warmest part of the refrigerator and eaten as soon as possible.)

MELON PURÉE

No cooking   *Calories: 120 (approx.) per melon*

Purée the required amount of melon to a smooth texture using an electric/hand blender, or mash finely with a fork.

To store: Melon purée is best made as required and eaten straightaway.

NECTARINE & PEACH
Nutrient content: Nectarines and peaches contain carbo-hydrate, minerals especially potassium, vitamin A, some of the B vitamins and a little vitamin C.
To buy: Look for plump fruit with a pleasant odour, which yield to gentle pressure.
To store: Store as for Apple, page 70. Ripe ones will keep for a few days.
To prepare: No special preparation.

NECTARINE/PEACH PURÉE
No cooking   *Calories: 35 (approx.) per whole fruit*
See Raw Apricot Purée, page 71, for method.

PEAR
Nutrient content: Pears contain carbohydrate, minerals especially potassium, vitamin A, some of the B vitamins and a little vitamin C.
To buy: Look for firm fruit with unblemished skins, and ripen at home. A pear is ready to eat when it will yield slightly to gentle pressure.
To store: Store as for Apple, page 70. Ripe ones will keep for a few days.
To prepare: Wash, quarter and core.

PEAR PURÉE
No cooking   *Calories: 40 (approx.) per pear*
Peel the required amount of pear thinly then purée to a smooth texture with an electric/hand blender, or mash finely with a fork. Alternatively, grate the prepared pear using the finest section of a cheese grater, discarding the skin as you do so. (Using an electric blender makes the smoothest purée.)
To store: This purée should be served straightaway.

PINEAPPLE
Nutrient content: Pineapples contain carbohydrate, minerals especially potassium, vitamin A, some of the B vitamins and vitamin C.
To buy: Look for firm, unblemished fruit which are heavy for

their size. When ripe, a leaf will pull easily from the crown.
To store: Pineapples should be stored at room temperature
until ripe and then eaten.
To prepare: Wash, cut off the leafy crown and cut crossways
into as many ½ inch (1cm) thick slices as required. Cut each
slice into cubes, removing the skin and eyes (the small round
areas of skin-like material in the pineapple's flesh just under
the main skin) and central core. (Any unused pineapple
should be wrapped tightly in polythene or foil and stored in
the warmest part of the refrigerator and eaten as soon as
possible.)

PINEAPPLE PURÉE
No cooking   *Calories: 12 (approx.) per 1 oz/25g*
Purée the required amount of prepared pineapple to a
smooth texture using an electric blender.

PLUM
Nutrient content: Plums contain carbohydrate, minerals
especially potassium, vitamin A, some of the B vitamins and a
very little vitamin C.
To buy: Look for plump fruit which yields slightly to gentle
pressure.
To store: Ripe plums are best stored loosely wrapped in a
polythene bag in the warmest part of the refrigerator, where
they will keep for a few days.
To prepare: Wash and remove stalks (if any).

RAW PLUM PURÉE (Using dessert plums.)
No cooking   *Calories: 15 (approx.) per plum*
See Raw Apricot Purée, page 71, for method.

COOKED PLUM PURÉE (Using cooking plums.)
                     Calories: 12 (approx.) per plum
Cooking time: 10 – 15 minutes
Put the required amount of plums into a suitable-sized
saucepan with just enough cold water to moisten the bottom
of the pan. Bring to the boil, lower the heat, cover with a
fitting lid and simmer for 10 minutes or until tender. Sweeten

to taste with a little unrefined sugar while still hot. Purée to a smooth texture by pushing through a sieve with the back of a spoon, discarding skins and stones.

PRUNE
Nutrient content: Prunes contain carbohydrate, minerals especially potassium, vitamin A and some of the B vitamins.
Availability: Moisturised and ready-to-eat dried pitted prunes are available from supermarkets.
To buy: Look for longest 'best by date' on pack.
To prepare: Wash in a colander or sieve under running cold water.

PRUNE PURÉE
Calories: 35 (approx.) per 1 oz/25g dry weight
Cooking time: 15 – 20 minutes
Place the required amount of prunes in a suitable-sized saucepan with just enough cold water to cover. Bring to the boil, lower the heat, cover with a fitting lid and simmer for about 15 minutes, or until the fruit is plump and tender. Drain the prunes through a sieve, reserving the cooking liquid. Purée to a smooth texture with an electric/hand blender, adding a little of the cooking liquid if a thinner consistency is required.

RAISIN & SULTANA
Nutrient content: Raisins and sultanas contain carbohydrate, minerals especially potassium, vitamin A, some of the B vitamins and a little vitamin E.
Availability: Ready-washed raisins and sultanas are available from supermarkets.
To buy: Look for longest 'best by date' on pack.
To store: Store in original unopened pack and transfer to an airtight container after opening.
To prepare: Wash in a sieve or colander under running cold water.

RAISIN SULTANA PURÉE
Calories: 70 (approx.) per 1 oz/25g dry weight
Cooking time: 15 – 20 minutes
Soak the required amount of raisins or sultanas overnight in

cold water. Place the fruit in a suitable-sized saucepan with just enough water to cover. Bring to the boil, lower the heat, cover with a fitting lid and simmer for about 15 minutes, or until the fruit is plump and tender. Drain the fruit through a sieve, reserving the cooking liquid. Purée to a smooth texture with an electric/hand blender, adding a little of the cooking liquid if a thinner consistency is required.

RHUBARB

Nutrient content: Rhubarb contains very little carbohydrate, minerals especially potassium and calcium, vitamin A, some of the B vitamins and vitamin C.

Availability: Rhubarb is available from winter to summer.

To buy: Choose rhubarb with fresh, firm stems and pink colouring.

To store: Rhubarb is best stored loosely wrapped in a polythene bag in the warmest part of the refrigerator where it will keep for a few days.

To prepare: Wash well under running cold water, trim ends and cut into 1 inch (2.5cm) lengths.

RHUBARB PURÉE

Calories: 2 (approx.) per 1 oz/25g

Cooking time: 10 minutes

Put the required amount of prepared fruit into a suitable-sized saucepan with just enough water to moisten the bottom of the pan. Bring up to simmering point, cover with a fitting lid and continue to simmer for 10 minutes or until the fruit is soft and mushy. Sweeten to taste with a little unrefined sugar, while the fruit is still hot (the heat should melt the sugar). Purée to a smooth texture using an electric blender.

TOMATO

Nutrient content: Tomatoes contain very little incomplete protein and carbohydrate, minerals especially potassium, vitamin A, some of the B vitamins and vitamin C.

To buy: Look for firm, unblemished light red tomatoes.

To store: Tomatoes are best stored in a paper bag or in a drawer at room temperature until ripe, when they should be

consumed, or lightly wrapped in a polythene bag and stored in the warmest part of the refrigerator, where they will keep for up to a week.
To prepare: Wash and quarter.

TOMATO PURÉE
No cooking   *Calories: 8 (approx.) per tomato*
Place the required amount of prepared tomatoes in a sieve and purée to a smooth texture by pushing through with the back of a spoon, discarding skin and seeds etc.

VEGETABLE PURÉES

ASPARAGUS
Nutrient content: Asparagus contains a little incomplete protein and carbohydrate, minerals especially potassium, vitamin A, some of the B vitamins, and vitamins C and E.
Availability: Asparagus is available from April to December.
To buy: Choose firm fresh-looking stalks, avoiding those that are limp-looking or have brown woody stems.
To store: Asparagus is best stored loosely wrapped in a polythene bag in the warmest part of the refrigerator, where it will keep for a few days.
To prepare: Wash quickly in running water, scrape lightly from top to bottom, and trim ends which may be tough.

ASPARAGUS PURÉE
Cooking time: 20 minutes   Calories: 5 (approx.) per spear
Preheat the oven to gas mark 4 (350°F/180°C). Wrap the required amount of prepared asparagus in lightly buttered foil and bake in the middle of the oven for about 20 minutes, or until tender. Purée to a smooth texture with an electric/hand blender, adding as much previously boiled water as necessary to achieve the desired consistency.

GEEEN BEAN (E.g. French, runner and broad.)
Nutrient content: Green beans contain a little incomplete protein and carbohydrate, minerals especially potassium,

vitamin A, some of the B vitamins and vitamin C.
To buy: Look for small, firm beans with a good colour. They should break with a crisp snap when bent.
To store: Green beans are best stored loosely wrapped in a polythene bag in the warmest part of the refrigerator where they will keep for up to a week.
To prepare: Wash beans in a colander under running cold water, trim ends and strings (if any) and cut into 1 inch (2.5cm) lengths.

GREEN BEAN PURÉE
Calories: 8 (approx.) per 1 oz/25g raw weight
Cooking time: 5 – 15 minutes
Put the required amount of prepared beans into a suitable-sized saucepan with enough cold water to come halfway up the sides. Bring to the boil, lower the heat, cover with a fitting lid and simmer for 5 to 15 minutes, or until tender. Drain through a sieve, reserving the cooking liquid. Purée to a smooth texture using an electric/hand blender, adding as much of the cooking liquid as necessary to get the required consistency.

DRIED BEAN (E.g. butter, haricot and kidney.)
Nutrient content: Dried beans contain incomplete protein, carbohydrate, a good amount of minerals and some of the B vitamins.
Availability: Dried beans are widely available in super-markets.
To buy: Buy from a source with a rapid turnover as very old beans can become tough.
To store: Store in original packs and transfer contents to an airtight container after opening. Correctly stored beans will usually keep for up to a year.
To prepare: Soak the beans in cold water overnight.

DRIED BEAN PURÉE
Calories: 75 (approx.) per 1 oz/25g raw weight
Cooking time: 1 – 1½ hours
Put the required amount of prepared drained beans into a

suitable-sized saucepan with plenty of cold water. Bring to
the boil, lower the heat, cover with a fitting lid and simmer for
1 to 1½ hours until tender. Drain through a sieve, reserving
the cooking liquid and purée to a smooth texture using an
electric/hand blender, or by pushing through a sieve with the
back of a spoon, adding as much of the cooking liquid as
necessary to achieve the desired consistency.

BEETROOT
Nutrient content: Beetroots contain a little incomplete
protein, carbohydrate, minerals especially potassium, some
of the B vitamins and vitamin C.
To buy: Buy small, firm beetroots, with undamaged skins.
To store: Fresh beetroots should be stored unwashed in a
vegetable rack in a dark, airy and cool place, if possible. They
will keep for 2 to 3 months at 50 – 55°F (10 – 13°C), but only
for about a week at room temperature.
To prepare: Wash carefully, taking care not to damage the
skin. Trim tops, if any, and root down to 1 inch (2.5cm).

BEETROOT PURÉE
                    Calories: 30 (approx.) per raw beetroot
Cooking time: 1 hour or more
Put the required amount of prepared beetroot into a suitable-
sized saucepan with plenty of cold water. Bring to the boil,
lower the heat, cover with a fitting lid and simmer until
cooked (i.e. when the skins will slide off easily when gently
rubbed). Remove the skins and purée to a smooth texture
using an electric/hand blender, or mash with a fork until
smooth, adding a little previously boiled water if a thinner
consistency is required.

BROCCOLI
Nutrient content: Broccoli contains a little incomplete
protein and carbohydrate, minerals especially potassium,
vitamin A, some of the B vitamins, vitamin C and a little
vitamin E.
To buy: Look for firm stalks with closely packed, well-
coloured heads.

To store: As for Asparagus, page 82.
To prepare: Trim stalks and leaves and wash well under running cold water.

BROCCOLI PURÉE
> *Calories: 7 (approx.) per 1 oz/25g raw weight*
Cooking time: 10 – 15 minutes
Put the required amount of prepared broccoli into a suitable-sized saucepan with enough cold water to come halfway up the sides. Bring to the boil, lower the heat, cover with a fitting lid and simmer for 10 to 15 minutes, or until tender. Drain through a sieve, reserving the cooking liquid. Purée to a smooth texture using an electric/hand blender, adding a little of the cooking liquid if a thinner consistency is required.

BRUSSELS SPROUT
Nutrient content: Brussels sprouts contain a little incomplete protein and carbohydrate, minerals especially potassium, vitamin A, some of the B vitamins, vitamin C and a little vitamin E.
Availability: Fresh sprouts are available in winter and spring.
To buy: Choose small sprouts which are bright green in colour and have a solid and closely packed appearance. Avoid sprouts with wilted leaves.
To store: As for Asparagus, page 82.
To prepare: Trim outer leaves and stem, and cut a deep cross in the base of the sprout (to enable the stem to cook at the same speed as the leaves) then wash in a colander under running cold water.

BRUSSELS SPROUT PURÉE
> *Calories: 7 (approx.) per 1 oz/25g raw weight*
Cooking time: 10 minutes
Put the required amount of prepared sprouts into a suitable-sized saucepan. Barely cover with cold water. Bring to the boil, lower the heat, cover with a fitting lid and simmer for 10 minutes, or until tender. Drain through a sieve, reserving the cooking liquid. Purée to a smooth texture using an electric/hand blender, adding a little of the cooking liquid if a thinner consistency is required.

CABBAGE (E.g. savoy, spring, white and winter.)
Nutrient content: Cabbage contains a little incomplete protein and carbohydrate, minerals especially potassium, vitamin A, some of the B vitamins and vitamin C.
To buy: Buy cabbages with fresh, crisp-looking leaves that are closely packed and heavy in comparison with their size.
To store: Cabbages should be stored loosely wrapped in a polythene bag in the warmest part of the refrigerator, where they will keep for up to 2 weeks.
To prepare: Discard any damaged leaves and coarse stalks, slice finely then wash well in a colander under running cold water.

CABBAGE PURÉE
　　　　　Calories: 7 (approx.) per 1 oz/25g raw weight
Cooking time: about 10 minutes
Put the required amount of prepared cabbage into a suitable-sized saucepan with enough cold water to come halfway up the sides. Bring to the boil, lower the heat, cover with a fitting lid and simmer for 10 minutes, or until tender. Drain through a sieve, reserving the cooking liquid. Purée to a smooth texture using an electric/hand blender, adding a little of the cooking liquid if a thinner consistency is required.

CARROT
Nutrient content: Carrots contain a little incomplete protein and carbohydrate, minerals, vitamin A, some of the B vitamins and a little vitamin C and E.
To buy: Choose firm, well-coloured carrots with smooth skins.
To store: As for Green Beans, page 83.
To prepare: Old carrots should be peeled, topped and tailed; young carrots can be well-scrubbed rather than peeled. Wash in running cold water and slice.

CARROT PURÉE
　　　　　Calories: 7 (approx.) per 1 oz/25g raw weight
Cooking time: 8 – 15 minutes, depending on size
Put the required amount of prepared carrots into a suitable-

sized saucepan with just enough cold water to cover. Bring to the boil, lower the heat, cover with a fitting lid and simmer for 8 minutes, or until tender. Drain through a sieve, reserving the cooking liquid. Purée to a smooth texture by mashing finely with a fork, adding a little of the cooking liquid if a thinner consistency is required.

CAULIFLOWER
Nutrient content: Cauliflower contains very little incomplete protein and carbohydrate, minerals especially potassium, a little vitamin A and C, and some of the B vitamins.
To buy: Choose cauliflowers with fresh, green-looking leaves and white closely packed heads.
To store: As for Green Beans, page 83.
To prepare: Discard outer, damaged leaves, trim stem, cut into wedges, and wash well in a colander under running cold water.

CAULIFLOWER PURÉE
> *Calories: 5 (approx.) per 1 oz/25g raw weight*
Cooking time: 10 – 15 minutes
Put the required amount of prepared cauliflower into a suitable-sized saucepan. Barely cover with cold water. Bring to the boil, lower the heat, cover with a fitting lid and simmer for 10 minutes, or until tender. Drain though a sieve, reserving the cooking liquid. Purée to a smooth texture using an electric/hand blender, adding a little of the cooking liquid if a thinner consistency is required.

CELERY
Nutrient content: Celery contains very little incomplete protein and carbohydrate, minerals and a little of the B vitamins and vitamin C and E.
To buy: Look for small to medium heads of celery with crisp-looking stalks.
To store: Celery should be stored loosely wrapped in a polythene bag in the warmest part of the refrigerator where it will keep for up to a week if uncut.
To prepare: Remove outer tough or blemished stalks if any.

Trim leaves and roots of stalks to be cooked, scrub well under running cold water, then slice.

CELERY PURÉE
> *Calories: 5 (approx.) per stick raw weight*
Cooking time: 15 – 20 minutes
Put the required amount of prepared celery into a suitable-sized saucepan with enough cold water to come halfway up the sides. Bring to the boil, lower the heat, cover with a fitting lid and simmer for 15 minutes, or until tender. Purée to a smooth texture using an electric/hand blender.

COURGETTE
Nutrient content: Courgettes contain very little incomplete protein and carbohydrate, minerals, a little vitamin A, B vitamins and vitamin C.
To buy: Look for small courgettes, with smooth, un-blemished, well-coloured skins.
To store: As for Green Beans, page 83.
To prepare: Wash well under running cold water, trim ends and slice.

COURGETTE PURÉE
> *Calories: 10 (approx.) per courgette*
Cooking time: 5 – 10 minutes
Put the required amount of prepared courgettes into a suitable-sized saucepan with enough cold water to come halfway up the sides. Bring to the boil, lower the heat, cover with a fitting lid and simmer for 5 to 10 minutes, or until tender. Purée to a smooth texture using an electric/hand blender.

LEEK
Nutrient content: Leeks contain a very little incomplete protein and carbohydrate, minerals especially potassium, vitamin A, some of the B vitamins, vitamin C and a little vitamin E.
Availability: Leeks are available in autumn and spring.

To buy: Look for small firm leeks with white roots and green tops.

To store: Leeks should be stored unwashed in a vegetable rack in a dark, airy and cool place, if possible.

To prepare: Trim root and leaves. Discard any outer coarse or damaged leaves. Slice in half lengthways and then crossways into ½ inch (1cm) lengths. Wash well under running cold water.

LEEK PURÉE

Cooking time: 5 minutes   Calories: 25 (approx.) per leek

Put the required amount of prepared leeks into a suitable-sized saucepan with enough cold water to come halfway up the sides. Bring to the boil, lower the heat, cover with a fitting lid and simmer for 5 minutes, or until tender. Drain through a sieve and purée to a smooth texture using an electric/hand blender.

LENTIL

Nutrient content: Lentils are a good source of incomplete protein and carbohydrate. They also contain minerals especially potassium, vitamin A and some of the B vitamins.

Availability: Lentils are widely available in supermarkets.

To buy: Buy from a source with a rapid turnover as old lentils can be tough.

To store: Store in original packs until opening and then transfer contents to an airtight container. Correctly stored lentils will usually keep for up to a year.

To prepare: Rinse in a sieve under running cold water.

LENTIL PURÉE

Calories: 85 (approx.) per 1 oz/25g raw weight
Cooking time: 30 minutes

Put the required amount of prepared lentils into a suitable-sized saucepan with plenty of cold water. Bring to the boil, lower the heat, cover with a fitting lid and simmer for 30 minutes or until soft. Drain through a sieve, reserving the cooking liquid and purée to a smooth texture using an electric/hand blender, or by pushing through a sieve with the back of a spoon, adding as much of the cooking liquid as necessary to achieve the desired consistency.

MUSHROOM
Nutrient content: Mushrooms contain a very little incomplete protein, minerals especially potassium, some of the B vitamins and a very little vitamin C.
To buy: Choose white unblemished button mushrooms.
To store: As for Asparagus, page 82.
To prepare: Wash well under running cold water.

MUSHROOM PURÉE
Calories: 5 (approx.) per 1 oz/25g raw weight
Cooking time: 5 minutes
Put the required amount of prepared mushrooms into a suitable-sized saucepan. Barely cover with cold water. Bring to the boil, lower the heat, cover with a fitting lid and simmer for 5 minutes, or until tender. Drain through a sieve and purée to a smooth texture using an electric/hand blender.

PARSNIP
Nutrient content: Parsnips contain very little incomplete protein, carbohydrate, minerals especially potassium, some of the B vitamins, vitamin C and a very little vitamin E.
To buy: Buy small, white, firm parsnips with as few blemishes as possible.
To store: As for Green Beans, page 83.
To prepare: Peel, top and tail, wash under running cold water, then slice.

PARSNIP PURÉE
Calories: 15 (approx.) per 1 oz/25g raw weight
Cooking time: 10 minutes
Put the required amount of prepared parsnips into a suitable-sized saucepan. Barely cover with cold water. Bring to the boil, lower the heat, cover with a fitting lid and simmer for 10 minutes, or until tender. Drain through a sieve, reserving the

cooking liquid. Purée to a smooth texture by mashing finely with a fork, adding as much of the cooking liquid as necessary to achieve the desired consistency.

PEA
Nutrient content: Peas contain a little incomplete protein and carbohydrate, minerals especially potassium, vitamin A, some of the B vitamins and vitamin C.
Availability: Fresh peas are available in the summer.
To buy: Look for small, crisp, well-filled pods.
To store: As for Asparagus, page 82.
To prepare: Shell and wash under running cold water.

PEA PURÉE
          Calories: 20 (approx.) per 1 oz/25g raw weight
Cooking time: 10 – 15 minutes
Put the required amount of prepared peas into a suitable-sized saucepan. Barely cover with cold water. Bring to the boil, lower the heat, cover with a fitting lid and simmer for 10 minutes, or until tender. Drain through a sieve, reserving the cooking liquid. Purée to a smooth texture using an electric/hand blender, adding a little of the cooking liquid if necessary to achieve the desired consistency.

POTATO & SWEET POTATO
Nutrient content: Potatoes contain very little incomplete protein, a fair amount of carbohydrate, minerals especially potassium, some of the B vitamins and vitamin C.
To buy: Look for well-formed, firm potatoes with unblemished skins.
To store: Potatoes should be stored unwashed in a vegetable rack in a dark, airy and cool place, if possible, where they will keep for 2 to 3 months. Potatoes stored at room temperature will only last for a week or so.
To prepare: Clean potatoes thoroughly by scrubbing them under running cold water, remove any eyes etc., but do not peel. Cut into 1 inch (2.5cm) dice.

POTATO PURÉE
Calories: 25 (approx.) per 1 oz/25g raw weight
Cooking time: 15 minutes
Put the required amount of prepared potatoes into a suitable-
sized saucepan. Barely cover with cold water. Bring to the
boil, lower the heat, cover with a fitting lid and simmer for 15
minutes, or until tender. Drain through a sieve, reserving the
cooking liquid. Remove the peel and then purée to a smooth
texture by mashing finely with a fork, adding a little of the
cooking liquid if a thinner consistency is required.

SPINACH

Nutrient content: Spinach contains very little incomplete
protein and carbohydrate, minerals especially calcium,
vitamin A, some of the B vitamins, vitamin C and a little
vitamin E.
To buy: Look for small, well-coloured, crisp-looking leaves
without blemishes.
To store: Spinach should be stored loosely wrapped in a
polythene bag in the warmest part of the refrigerator where it
will keep for up to 2 days.
To prepare: Cut away any coarse stalks and damaged leaves
then wash well under running cold water. The leaves may be
rolled up and sliced to make them more manageable, if
desired.

SPINACH PURÉE
Calories: 10 (approx.) per 1 oz/25g cooked weight
Cooking time: 5 – 10 minutes
Put the required amount of prepared spinach with the water
that clings to it after washing (no additional liquid is
required) into a suitable-sized saucepan. Bring to the boil,
lower the heat, cover with a fitting lid and simmer for 5
minutes, or until tender. Drain through a sieve, reserving the
cooking liquid and purée to a smooth texture with an
electric/hand blender, adding a little of the cooking liquid if a
thinner consistency is required.

SPRING GREEN

Nutrient content: Spring greens contain very little incomplete protein and carbohydrate, minerals especially potassium, vitamin A, some of the B vitamins, vitamin C and a very little vitamin E.

To buy: Look for firm, well-coloured, undamaged leaves.

To store: Greens should be stored loosely wrapped in a polythene bag in the warmest part of the refrigerator where they will keep for up to 3 days.

To prepare: Cut away stalks and any damaged leaves, roll up each leaf and cut into ½ inch (1cm) slices (to make it more manageable).

SPRING GREEN PURÉE

Calories: 3 (approx.) per 1 oz/25g cooked weight
Cooking time: 8 – 10 minutes

Put the required amount of prepared greens into a suitable-sized saucepan with enough cold water to come about halfway up the sides. Bring to the boil, lower the heat, cover with a fitting lid and simmer for about 8 minutes or until tender. Drain through a sieve, reserving the cooking liquid. Purée to a smooth texture using an electric/hand blender, adding a little of the cooking liquid if a thinner consistency is required.

SWEDE

Nutrient content: Swedes contain a very little incomplete protein and carbohydrate, minerals especially potassium, some of the B vitamins and vitamin C.

To buy: Look for small, undamaged swedes.

To store: Swedes should ideally be stored in a vegetable rack in a dark, airy and cool place (50 – 55°F/10 – 13°C) where they will keep for 2 to 3 months. They will last a week or so at room temperature.

To prepare: Peel thickly, wash and cut into 1 inch (2.5cm) dice.

SWEDE PURÉE

Calories: 5 (approx.) per 1 oz/25g raw weight
Cooking time: 15 minutes

Put the required amount of prepared swede into a suitable-

sized saucepan. Barely cover with cold water. Bring to the
boil, lower the heat, cover with a fitting lid and simmer for
about 15 minutes, or until tender. Drain through a sieve,
reserving the cooking liquid. Purée to a smooth texture by
mashing finely with a fork, adding a little of the cooking
liquid if a thinner consistency is required.

TURNIP
Nutrient content: Turnips contain very little incomplete
protein, fat and carbohydrate, minerals especially potassium,
some of the B vitamins and vitamin C.
To buy: Look for small, well-formed turnips with whitish
unblemished skins.
To store: Turnips should be stored unwashed in a vegetable
rack in a dark, airy and cool place, if possible, where they will
keep for 2 to 3 months. Turnips stored at room temperature
will only last for up to a week.
To prepare: Peel and cut into 1 inch (2.5cm) dice.

TURNIP PURÉE
        Calories: 6 (approx.) per 1 oz/25g raw weight
Cooking time: 15 minutes
Put the required amount of prepared turnips into a suitable-
sized saucepan and barely cover with cold water. Bring to the
boil, lower the heat, cover with a fitting lid and simmer for 15
minutes, or until tender. Drain through a sieve, reserving the
cooking liquid. Purée to a smooth texture by mashing finely
with a fork, adding a little of the cooking liquid if a thinner
consistency is required.

PART THREE

RECIPES FOR
OLD HANDS

(6 months onwards)

8. MEAT, FISH, EGG AND DAIRY FOOD PURÉES

All the meat and fish purées may be stored in a refrigerator for up to 24 hours or frozen for up to a month. The egg and dairy food purées are best freshly made as required.

MEAT
Nutrient content: All meat contains complete protein, fat, minerals, all the B vitamins and a little vitamin E. Liver and kidney also contain vitamins A and C; and liver is a source of vitamin D.

To buy: The type of cut you buy will depend on your method of cooking. There is little advantage in buying expensive cuts of meat for puréeing, because cheaper cuts are equal in nutritional value and can become as tender if a slow moist method of cooking is used.

Always buy the freshest meat available from a reliable butcher or good supermarket (look for the longest 'sell by date' when buying pre-packed meat).

Choose red meat or veal which is firm and elastic to touch, moist but not wet, and as free from visible fat as possible. Any fluid should be watery and not sticky and there should be very little odour. The same general rules apply to cuts of poultry, except that they should be completely odour-free. Whole birds should look plump and well-rounded with a skin free from blemishes and bruising. Liver should be very dark in colour with little odour.

To store: All raw meat and poultry should be cleaned quickly under running cold water, patted dry with paper kitchen towel, placed in the coolest part of the refrigerator on a clean plate, loosely covered with polythene or foil. Most types of meat will keep for two to five days, except minced meat and offal, which are more perishable, and should only be stored for one to two days.

N.B. Any freshly cooked meat you have prepared for the rest of the family can be puréed for your baby, providing it has been cooked without the addition of too much fat or salt.

MEAT PURÉE NUMBER ONE (Using lean minced beef, lamb or veal.)

Calories: 40 (approx.) per 1 oz/25g raw weight
Cooking time: 15 – 20 minutes

Toss and separate the meat in its own fat in a saucepan over a moderate heat until the fat runs out and the meat is lightly browned, but still soft. Then drain well on paper kitchen towel. Return the meat to the pan with just enough water to cover, bring to the boil, lower the heat, cover with a fitting lid and simmer for 10 to 15 minutes, or until the meat is tender.

Drain the meat through a sieve, reserving the cooking liquid. Purée to a smooth texture with an electric/hand blender, adding as much of the cooking liquid as necessary to achieve the desired consistency.

To serve: Serve with mixed vegetables.

MEAT PURÉE NUMBER TWO (Using lean stewing beef, veal or lamb.)

Calories: 40 (approx.) per 1 oz/25g raw weight
Cooking time: 1½ hours or more

Cut the meat into ½ inch (1cm) dice and place in a suitable-sized saucepan with just enough cold water to cover. Bring up to the boil, lower the heat, cover with a fitting lid and simmer for 1½ hours or until tender. Drain and purée as in Meat Purée Number One.

To serve: Serve with mixed vegetables.

POULTRY PURÉE (Using skinned and boned chicken or turkey meat.)

Calories: 35 (approx.) per 1 oz/25g raw weight
Cooking time: 30 minutes

Cut the meat into ½ inch (1cm) dice and place in a suitable-sized saucepan with just enough cold water to cover. Bring to the boil, lower the heat, cover with a fitting lid and simmer for half an hour or until tender. Drain and purée as in Meat Purée Number One.

To serve: Serve with mixed vegetables.

LIVER PURÉE (Using lamb's liver.)

Calories: 50 (approx.) per 1 oz/25g raw weight
Cooking time: 10 minutes

Cut the liver into large, even-sized pieces and place in a suitable-sized saucepan with just enough cold water to cover. Bring to the boil, lower the heat, cover with a fitting lid and simmer for 10 minutes or until tender. (It is important not to overcook liver as it becomes tough.) Drain and purée as in Meat Purée Number One.

To serve: Serve with mixed vegetables.

KIDNEY PURÉE (Using lamb's kidney.)

Calories: 25 (approx.) per 1 oz/25g raw weight
Cooking time: 10 – 15 minutes

Remove the fat, skin and core from the kidney, cut into ¼ inch (½cm) thick slices and place in a suitable-sized saucepan with just enough cold water to cover. Bring to the boil, lower the heat, cover with a fitting lid and simmer for 10 to 15 minutes or until tender. Drain and purée as in Meat Purée Number One.

To serve: Serve with mixed vegetables.

FISH

Nutrient content: All fish contain complete protein, some B vitamins and minerals. Oily fish also contain fat and, therefore, varying amounts of vitamins A and D. The edible bones of tinned fish are a rich source of calcium and phosphorus.

To buy: Only buy fish which is absolutely fresh from a reliable fishmonger or good supermarket. White fish should look freshly cut with moist, plump, firm-textured flesh. There should be no signs of dryness or discolouration and any smell should be mild and clean. Oily fish such as salmon, tuna and sardines, are conveniently available ready-cooked, in tins.

To store: Fresh white fish should be cleaned quickly under running cold water, patted dry with paper kitchen towel, put in the coolest part of the refrigerator on a clean plate, covered loosely with polythene or foil. It is best eaten on day of purchase, but will keep until the next day, if necessary.

N.B. Any freshly cooked fish you have prepared for the rest of the family (with the exception of shellfish) can be puréed for your baby, providing it has been cooked without the addition of too much fat or salt.

WHITE FISH PURÉE (Using skinned and boned white fish.)
　　　　Calories: 25 (approx.) per 1 oz/25g raw weight
Cooking time: 3 – 4 minutes
N.B. Monk-fish is a good fish to use in baby recipes because once the central cartilage is removed (which the fishmonger can do) it is completely free from bones. This saves having to check laboriously for stray bones and agonising over any you may have missed with every mouthful baby takes!

Break or cut the fish into small pieces and put into a suitable-sized saucepan with just enough water or milk to cover. Bring just up to boiling point, lower the heat and simmer very gently, uncovered, for 3 to 4 minutes or until the fish is tender.

Drain the fish through a sieve, reserving the cooking liquid. Purée to a smooth texture using an electric/hand blender, adding as much of the cooking liquid as necessary to achieve the desired consistency.

To serve: Serve with mixed vegetables.

OILY FISH PURÉE (Using tinned and drained salmon, tuna, sardines, pilchards or mackerel.)

No cooking   *Calories: 50 (approx.) per 1 oz/25g*

Purée the fish to a smooth texture using an electric/hand blender, or mash very finely with a fork, adding as much water or milk as necessary to achieve the desired consistency.

To serve: Serve with mixed vegetables.

EGGS

Nutrient content: Eggs are a good source of complete protein, fat, minerals and some of the B vitamins. Yolk also contains vitamins A and D.

To buy: Eggs are sold by size, graded from the smallest, size 7, to the largest, size 1. Buy the freshest eggs you can find. Boxes frequently carry a 'packing date' and 'sell by date' which are good guides to their freshness. Otherwise buy from a reliable source with a large turnover. To test an egg for freshness at home, place it in a vessel of cold water. If it lies horizontally on the bottom it is very fresh, if tilted or suspended it is not quite so new, if it floats it is stale. Always reserve the freshest eggs for boiling, poaching, etc., and use older eggs for making cakes, etc. Never buy eggs with cracked or dirty shells and discard any which have an 'off' odour when cracked or shelled.

To store: Eggs should be stored, pointed end down, away from strong-smelling foods in a pantry or refrigerator (where they will keep for longer).

EGG YOLK PURÉE

Calories 70 (approx.) per yolk
Cooking time: a few seconds
Place the required amount of egg yolk in a small ramekin and
stand it for a few seconds in a larger dish of water that has just
been boiled, until the yolk is warmed slightly and beginning
to thicken. Thin down the yolk if necessary, with a little water
or milk.
To serve: Serve with bread and butter or toast.

WHOLE EGG PURÉE

Calories 90 (approx.) per egg
Cooking time: about 4 minutes
Put the required amount of eggs into a suitable-sized
saucepan with cold water to cover. Bring to the boil, lower the
heat, and boil gently for 3 minutes – there is no need to use a
lid. Shell each egg, scoop out contents, and purée to a smooth
texture by mashing finely with a fork, adding a little water or
milk if a thinner consistency is required.
To serve: Serve with bread and butter or toast.   :

CHEDDAR CHEESE
Nutrient content: Cheese is a good source of complete
protein, fat, minerals especially calcium, vitamins A and D
and some of the B vitamins.

To buy: Generally, cheddar cheese should have a smooth mat
appearance. Avoid cheese which looks cracked or sweaty as
this means it is drying out due to long exposure to the air.
Look out for the longest 'sell by date' when buying pre-
packed cheese in a supermarket.
To store: Cheese will keep for up to 2 weeks in the refrigerator
wrapped in polythene or foil.

CHEDDAR CHEESE PURÉE
No cooking   *Calories: 120 (approx.) per 1 oz/25g*
Finely grate the required amount of cheese and mix well with

as much boiling water or milk as necessary, to achieve the desired consistency.

YOGHURT
Nutrient content: Low fat yoghurt is a source of complete protein, carbohydrate, minerals especially potassium and a little vitamin A. Low fat yoghurt is sometimes fortified with extra vitamin A and vitamin D.

To buy: Buy natural unsweetened yoghurt for baby or artificial-additive-free fruit varieties. The longer the 'sell by date' on the carton, the fresher the yoghurt.

To store: Yoghurt should be stored in a refrigerator and consumed by the date given on the carton.

YOGHURT PURÉE (Using natural, unsweetened yoghurt.)
No cooking   *Calories: 15 (approx.) per 1 oz/25g*
Simply remove the required amount of yoghurt from the carton, thin down a little with water or milk, if necessary, and serve.

COTTAGE CHEESE
Nutrient content: Cottage cheese is a source of complete protein, a little fat and carbohydrate, minerals, vitamin A and some of the B vitamins.

To buy: Always buy natural, artificial-additive-free cottage cheese with the longest 'sell by date' possible.

To store: Cottage cheese may be stored in a refrigerator for as long as directed on the carton.

COTTAGE CHEESE PURÉE
No cooking   *Calories: 25 (approx.) per 1 oz/25g*
Remove the required amount of cottage cheese from the carton and purée until smooth with an electric/hand blender or push through a sieve with the back of a spoon, adding a little water or milk to get a thinner consistency if necessary.

9. BREAKFAST IDEAS

All these dishes are best eaten straightaway.

PLUM TOMATO SCRAMBLE
Cooking time: 3 – 4 minutes   *Calories: 160 (approx.)*

Small knob of butter
1 size 2 egg, lightly beaten with a fork
1 tinned plum tomato, roughly chopped

Melt the butter over a moderate heat in a small (preferably non-stick) milk pan until hot and frothy. Lower the heat slightly, then add the egg and tomato. Cook until the egg is just scrambled (i.e. just set but still soft), stirring all the time to prevent sticking.
To serve: For younger babies, mash with a fork if necessary. Serve with bread and butter, or toast.

PORRIDGE AND BANANA
Cooking time: a few minutes   *Calories: 195 (approx.)*

3 tbsp porridge oats
6 tbsp milk
½ small banana

Place the oats and milk in a small, preferably non-stick, milk pan and bring just up to simmering point, stirring occasionally. Lower the heat and simmer gently, uncovered, for about 3 minutes. The porridge should be thick and creamy.

To serve: For younger babies, purée the porridge and banana to the desired texture with an electric/hand blender, adding a little previously boiled milk or water if a thinner consistency is required. For older babies, mash or chop the banana and mix with the porridge, thin with a little milk if necessary and serve.

MUESLI
No cooking   *Calories: 30 per tablespoon (approx.)*

Oatmeal (4 parts)
Wheatgerm (2 parts)
Ground hazelnuts (1 part)
Ground almonds (1 part)
Desiccated coconut (1 part)

Muesli made up in larger quantities than required may be stored in an airtight container for up to 1 month.
   Put the required amount of muesli into a bowl and mix to a purée of the desired consistency with a little milk, fruit juice, or natural unsweetened yoghurt. Top with puréed or chopped fresh fruit, or dried fruit (soaked or puréed first, if necessary) if liked.

OAT AND APPLE BREAKFAST
No cooking   *Calories: 130 (approx.)*

1 dessert apple, quartered, cored and peeled
1 rounded tbsp fine oatmeal
1 rounded tsp wheatgerm
Milk to mix

Purée the apple with an electric blender until smooth then mix with the oatmeal and wheatgerm adding as much milk as necessary to achieve the right consistency. (This method makes the smoothest purée.)

Alternatively, mix the oatmeal with the wheatgerm, grate in the apple (using the finest section of a cheese grater) and mix it all together with a little milk.

CHEESE ON BEANS ON TOAST
Cooking time: a few minutes   *Calories: 175 (approx.)*

2 heaped tbsp baked beans, mashed with a little juice from the tin
1 large slice of wholemeal bread, toasted if liked on one side only
½ oz (12g) cheddar cheese, grated

Mash the beans with a fork and spread evenly over the bread. Sprinkle with the cheese and place under a hot grill until the cheese melts.
To serve: Remove crusts, if not liked, and cut into suitable-sized pieces for baby to feed himself (½ – 1 inch/1 – 2.5cm squares at first).

FRENCH TOAST
Cooking time: a few minutes   *Calories: 220 (approx.)*

1 size 2 egg, lightly beaten with a fork
Pinch of mixed herbs (optional)
1 large slice of wholemeal bread
Small knob of butter

Mix the egg and herbs. Put the egg on a large plate and soak
the bread in it for a few minutes, or until all the egg has been
absorbed. Melt the butter over a high heat in a small
(preferably non-stick) frying pan. When hot and frothy,
reduce the heat slightly and fry the bread in it until slightly
golden on each side.
To serve: Remove the crusts if not liked. Cut the toast into
suitable-sized pieces ($\frac{1}{2}$ – 1 inch/ 1 – 2.5cm) and allow baby to
feed himself.

SUNRISE YOGHURT
No cooking   *Calories: 170 (approx.)*

4 tbsp natural unsweetened yoghurt
1 tbsp fruit juice of your choice
1 tbsp fine oatmeal
4 moisturised and ready-to-eat dried apricots
$\frac{1}{2}$ small banana
1 tsp ground hazelnuts

Purée all the ingredients with an electric blender.

LEFT-OVER OMELETTE
Cooking time: a few minutes   *Calories: 170 (approx.)*

1 small knob of butter
1 heaped tbsp cooked chopped vegetables of your choice
1 size 2 egg, beaten

Melt the butter over a high heat in a small (preferably non-stick) milk pan. When hot and frothy, add the vegetables and fry over a moderate heat until lightly browned. Add the egg and cook until the underside begins to set. Then with a wooden spoon or spatula draw the edges of the omelette towards the centre, allowing any liquid egg to run into the channels created. The omelette is cooked when the egg is no longer runny, but should still be quite moist on top. Flip the omelette in half and slide it out on to a plate.

To serve: Chop roughly into bite-size pieces. Serve with bread and butter.

BREAKFAST COCKTAIL
No cooking   *Calories: 185 (approx.)*

4 fl oz (112ml) orange juice
1 size 2 egg yolk
2 tbsp dried milk powder

Purée all the ingredients together with an electric blender or whisk with a balloon whisk, until light and frothy.

GRATED PEAR
No cooking   *Calories: 75 (approx.)*

1 ripe dessert pear, washed, quartered and cored
Few drops of lemon juice
1 level tbsp ground hazelnuts or almonds

Grate the pear flesh on the finest section of a cheese grater, discarding the skin as you do so. Mix well with the lemon juice and nuts and serve immediately.

10. SIMPLE SOUPS

SCOTCH BROTH
Cooking time: 1½ hours   *Calories: 140 (approx.)*

2 oz (50g) lean minced lamb
½ small onion, chopped
1 small carrot, chopped
½ small turnip, cut into ½ inch (1cm) dice
1 tbsp pot barley
Just enough water to cover the ingredients
Wheatgerm (for older babies, optional)

In a suitable-sized non-stick saucepan toss and separate the meat in its own fat over a moderate heat, until the fat runs out and the meat is lightly browned all over, but still soft. Then drain well on paper kitchen towel.

Return the meat to the pan with the rest of the ingredients except the wheatgerm. Bring to boiling point, lower the heat, cover with a fitting lid and simmer gently for 1½ hours.

To serve: For younger babies, strain the meat and vegetables

Scotch broth (contd)
through a sieve, reserving the cooking liquid for stock. Purée to the desired consistency with an electric blender, adding as much stock as necessary for a creamy texture.

For older babies, reduce the liquid, if necessary, by pouring off or boiling down. Thicken (if liked) by adding a little wheatgerm (see below) while the broth is gently simmering, stirring all the time until the sauce thickens.

To store: This dish may be stored in a refrigerator for up to 24 hours or frozen for up to 1 month.

N.B. If this dish is to be reheated after freezing, omit the wheatgerm at the cooking stage and add as required on reheating.

LENTIL SOUP
Cooking time: 30 minutes   *Calories: 80 (approx.)*

2 rounded tbsp red lentils
½ small onion, finely chopped
1 small carrot, finely diced
Tiny sprinkle of thyme
Just enough water to cover the ingredients

Put all the ingredients into a suitable-sized saucepan. Bring to the boil, lower the heat, cover with a fitting lid and simmer for 30 minutes or until the lentils are soft.

To serve: Strain the vegetables through a sieve, reserving the cooking liquid for stock. Purée to a smooth texture with an electric/hand blender, or push through a sieve with the back of a spoon, adding as much stock as necessary to achieve the desired consistency.

To store: Store as for Scotch Broth, above.

CREAM OF SWEDE SOUP
Cooking time: 20 minutes   *Calories: 50 (approx.)*

A small piece of swede, cut into ½ inch (1cm) dice
Just enough milk to cover the swede

Place the swede and milk in a small milk pan, bring just up to simmering point, lower the heat and continue to simmer uncovered for 15 to 20 minutes, or until the swede is tender and cooked.

To serve: Strain the swede through a sieve, reserving the cooking liquid for stock. Purée to a smooth texture by mashing with a fork, adding as much stock as necessary to achieve a creamy consistency.
To store: Store as for Scotch Broth, page 110.

FRESH TOMATO SOUP
Cooking time: 15 minutes   *Calories: 65 (approx.)*

½ small onion, sliced
1 small carrot, sliced
Tiny piece of bay leaf (optional)
Just enough milk to cover the ingredients
2 medium tomatoes, puréed as on page 82

Put the onion, carrot, bay leaf (if used) and milk into a small milk pan. Bring just up to simmering point, lower the heat and continue to simmer very gently, uncovered, for 15 minutes, stirring occasionally. Drain through a sieve, discarding the vegetables and bay leaf, reserving 3 tbsp of stock.

To serve: Stir the puréed tomatoes into the hot stock and serve immediately.
To store: This dish is best eaten straightaway.

VEGETABLE BROTH
Cooking time: 20 minutes   *Calories: 60 (approx.)*

1 small carrot, thinly sliced
1 small parsnip, thinly sliced
½ small onion, finely chopped
1 small stick of celery, thinly sliced

Vegetable Broth—contd.

½ small leek, cut in half lengthways and thinly sliced
½ small turnip, cut into ½ inch (1cm) dice
Just enough water to cover the ingredients

Put all the ingredients into a suitable-sized saucepan. Bring to
the boil, lower the heat, cover with a fitting lid and simmer
gently for 15 to 20 minutes, or until all the vegetables are
cooked.

To serve: Strain the vegetables through a sieve, reserving the
cooking liquid for stock. Purée to a smooth texture with an
electric/hand blender, or push through a sieve with the back
of a spoon, adding as much stock as necessary to achieve a
creamy consistency.
To store: Store as for Scotch Broth, page 110.

CREAMY SPINACH SOUP
Cooking time: 7 minutes   *Calories: 190 (approx.)*

2 oz (50g) fresh spinach
4 fl oz (122ml) milk
2 level tsp butter
4 level tsp flour

Wash the spinach well under running cold water, then shake
to remove as much of the moisture as you can. Remove the
centre stalk and any blemished leaves, and break into small
pieces. Purée the spinach and milk with an electric blender
until almost smooth.

   Place all the ingredients in a small milk pan and whisk with
a balloon whisk over a medium heat until the soup bubbles
and thickens, then lower the heat and simmer very gently,
uncovered, for about 7 minutes. Whisk again quickly when
cooked to remove the skin and serve.

To store: This dish is best eaten straightaway.

LEEK AND POTATO SOUP
Cooking time: 20 minutes   *Calories: 60 (approx.)*

1 small potato, cut into ½ inch (1cm) dice
½ small leek, cut in half lengthways and thinly sliced
1 small stick of celery, thinly sliced
Just enough water to cover the ingredients

See Vegetable Broth, opposite, for the method.
To serve: As for Vegetable Broth, opposite.
To store: Store as for Scotch Broth, page 110.

PRESSURE-COOKED BUTTER BEAN AND ONION SOUP
                                    Calories: 160 (approx.)
Cooking time: 15 minutes at high pressure

2 oz (50g) butter beans
½ small onion, sliced
½ small bay leaf
½ pint (285ml) water

Place the beans in a bowl. Pour over enough boiling water to cover well and leave to stand for 1 hour.

Drain the beans and put into the pressure cooker with the other ingredients. Bring to a rolling boil (i.e. gently boiling but not rising) in the open pan, cover with lid and bring up to pressure without altering the heat. Time the soup for 15 minutes from the time the cooker is up to pressure. Release steam slowly.

To serve: Discard the bay leaf. Strain the butter beans and onion through a sieve, reserving the cooking liquid for stock. Blend with an electric/hand blender, or push through a sieve with the back of a spoon, adding as much stock as necessary to achieve a creamy consistency.
To store: Store as for Scotch Broth, page 110.

THICK PEA SOUP
Cooking time: 20 minutes   *Calories: 20 (approx.)*

½ **small onion, finely chopped**
Just enough water to cover the ingredients
2 rounded tbsp frozen peas

Place the onion and water into a suitable-sized saucepan,
bring to the boil, lower the heat, cover with a fitting lid and
simmer for 15 minutes, then add the peas and a little more
water, if necessary. Bring up to boiling point once again,
lower the heat, cover with the lid and simmer for a further 3
minutes.

To serve: Strain the vegetables through a sieve, reserving the
cooking liquid for stock. Purée to a smooth texture with an
electric/hand blender, or push through a sieve with the back
of a spoon, adding as much stock as necessary to achieve a
creamy consistency.
To store: Store as for Scotch Broth, page 110.

COLD CHEESE AND CUCUMBER SOUP
No cooking   *Calories: 150 (approx.)*

½ **inch (1cm) chunk of cucumber, peeled**
1 oz (25g) cottage cheese
1 oz (25g) cheddar cheese, cut into small pieces

Purée all the ingredients to a smooth texture with an
electric/hand blender, adding a little milk if a thinner
consistency is desired.

To serve: Serve with bread and butter for babies whose
appetites demand it.
To store: This dish is best eaten straightaway.

MINESTRONE SOUP
Cooking time: 20 minutes   *Calories: 70 (approx.)*

½ small leek, cut in half lengthways and thinly sliced
½ small onion, finely chopped
½ small carrot, chopped
½ small stick of celery, chopped
3 green beans, cut into small crossways slices
1 tbsp baked beans (optional)
1 tbsp broken wholewheat macaroni
2 tbsp tomato juice
Pinch of basil
Just enough water to cover the ingredients
A little grated cheddar or Parmesan cheese (optional)

Put all the ingredients, except the cheese, into a suitable-sized saucepan and bring to the boil. Lower the heat, cover with a fitting lid, and simmer for 20 minutes, or until all the vegetables are cooked.

To serve: For younger babies, strain the vegetables through a sieve, reserving the cooking liquid for stock. Purée to the desired texture with an electric/hand blender, or mash/chop as necessary, adding as much stock as required to achieve the desired consistency. For older babies, reduce the liquid, if necessary, by pouring off or boiling down. For all babies, sprinkle with a little finely grated cheese, if liked.
To store: Store as for Scotch Broth, page 110.

FISH AND SWEETCORN SOUP
Cooking time: 20 minutes   *Calories: 95 (approx.)*

2 oz (50g) boneless white fish, skinned and cut into cubes
½ small onion, finely chopped
2 tbsp frozen sweetcorn
Just enough milk to cover the ingredients
Baby rice (for older babies, optional)

Place all the ingredients except the baby rice in a small milk pan, bring just up to simmering point, lower the heat, and continue to simmer very gently for 20 minutes.

To serve: For younger babies, strain the fish and vegetables through a sieve, reserving the cooking liquid for stock. Purée to the desired texture with an electric/hand blender, adding as much stock as necessary to achieve a creamy consistency.

For older babies, pour off any surplus liquid and thicken the rest (if liked) by stirring in a little baby rice (see below) while the soup is still hot.

To store: This dish may be stored in a refrigerator for up to 24 hours or frozen for up to 1 month.

N.B. If this soup is to be reheated after freezing, omit the baby rice at the cooking stage and add as required on reheating.

11. EGG DISHES

All these dishes are best eaten straightaway unless specified otherwise in the recipes.

EGG EN COCOTTE (Steamed egg)
Cooking time: 5 minutes   *Calories: 90 (approx.)*

1 size 2 egg

Crack the egg into a lightly buttered ramekin and place in a saucepan with enough cold water to come halfway up the side of the dish. Bring the water just up to boiling point, lower the heat, cover with a fitting lid and simmer the egg for 5 minutes or until lightly set.

To serve: For younger babies, mash or not as necessary. Serve with bread and butter or toast.

BAKED EGG
Cooking time: 15 – 20 minutes   *Calories: 90 (approx.)*

1 size 2 egg

Preheat the oven to gas mark 4 (350° F/180° C). Crack the egg into a lightly buttered ramekin and place a small knob of butter on top of the yolk. Bake for 15 minutes in the centre of the oven or until the egg is lightly set.

To serve: For younger babies, mash a little with a fork if necessary. Serve with bread and butter or toast.

EGG AND TOMATO PURÉE
No cooking   *Calories: 85 (approx.)*

**1 size 2 egg yolk, hard-boiled, shelled and sliced
1 medium tomato, quartered**

Push the egg and tomato through a sieve with the back of a spoon, mix well and serve.

To serve: Serve with bread and butter or toast.

SPINACH SCRAMBLE
Cooking time: 3 – 4 minutes   *Calories: 150 (approx.)*

**4 or 5 spinach leaves
1 size 2 egg
Small knob of butter**

Wash the spinach well under running cold water, then shake to remove most of the moisture. Remove the centre stalk and any blemished leaves, then break into small pieces. Purée the spinach and egg with an electric blender until almost smooth.
  Melt the butter over a moderate heat in a small (preferably non-stick) milk pan until hot and frothy. Lower the heat

slightly, add the egg mixture and cook until lightly scrambled (i.e. just set but still soft), stirring all the time to prevent sticking.

To serve: For younger babies, mash with a fork if necessary. Serve with bread and butter or toast.

EGGY MASH
Cooking time: 15 minutes   *Calories: 120 (approx.)*

1 small potato cut into $\frac{1}{2}$ inch (1cm) dice
Just enough water to cover the potato
1 size 2 egg yolk

Put the potato and water into a small saucepan and bring to the boil. Lower the heat, cover with a fitting lid and simmer for 15 minutes, or until cooked.

To serve: Drain the potato through a sieve, reserving the cooking liquid. Mash with the egg yolk, adding a little of the cooking liquid, if the purée is too thick.
To store: This dish may be stored in the refrigerator for up to 24 hours or frozen for up to 1 month.

EGG AND BEAN DINNER
Cooking time: 3 minutes   *Calories: 220 (approx.)*

1 size 2 egg, or yolk only, lightly beaten
3 rounded tbsp baked beans
1 slice wholemeal bread, crusts removed and cut into $\frac{1}{2}$ inch (1cm) squares

Place all the ingredients in a suitable-sized saucepan and warm the contents over a gentle heat for 1 to 2 minutes, stirring all the time, without boiling.

To serve: For younger babies, purée to the required texture with an electric/hand blender, or mash with a fork, adding a little milk if a thinner consistency is required. For older babies, serve as it is.

To store: This dish may be stored in a refrigerator for up to 24 hours or frozen for up to 1 month.

EGG, CHEESE AND TOMATO SAVOURY
Cooking time: 25 minutes   *Calories: 160 (approx.)*

1 size 2 egg
2 tbsp tomato juice
2 oz (50g) cottage cheese, sieved

Preheat the oven to gas mark 5 (375° F/190° C). Place all the ingredients in a small bowl and beat them together with a fork. Turn the mixture into a small, lightly buttered ovenproof dish and bake in the middle of the oven for about 20 to 25 minutes, or until the mixture is lightly set and the top is risen and golden.

To serve: For younger babies, mash with a fork, if necessary. Serve with bread and butter.

EGG AND CHEESE BAKE
Cooking time: 15 minutes   *Calories: 330 (approx.)*

2 oz (50g) cheddar cheese, finely grated
1 size 2 egg

Preheat the oven to gas mark 4 (350° F/180° C). Place half of the cheese in a lightly buttered ramekin, or similar-sized ovenproof dish. Break the egg carefully on to the cheese, then sprinkle the remaining cheese on top. Bake for 15 minutes in the centre of the oven until the cheese has melted and the egg is lightly set.

To serve: For younger babies, mash a little with a fork, if necessary. Serve with bread and butter.

EGG AND MARMITE TOAST
Cooking time: a few minutes   *Calories: 220 (approx.)*

1 size 2 egg, lightly beaten with a fork
A little Marmite
1 large slice of wholemeal bread
Small knob of butter

Put the egg on a large plate. Spread Marmite *very thinly* on
each side of the bread, then soak the bread in the egg for a few
minutes, or until all the egg is absorbed. Melt the butter over
a high heat in a small (preferably non-stick) frying pan. When
hot and frothy, reduce the heat slightly and fry the bread until
golden on each side.

To serve: Remove the crusts if not liked. Cut the toast into
suitable-sized pieces (½ to 1 inch/1 to 2.5 cm at first) and
allow baby to feed himself.

EGG AND TUNA BAKE
Cooking time: 20 – 30 minutes   *Calories: 190 (approx.)*

1 size 2 egg
1 tbsp milk
1 oz (25g) tinned tuna, drained and mashed
1 tbsp cooked peas or sweetcorn
1 heaped tbsp cheddar cheese, grated

Preheat the oven to gas mark 5 (375° F/190° C). Beat the egg
and milk together lightly with a fork. Put the mashed tuna,
peas or sweetcorn into a small lightly buttered ovenproof
dish. Sprinkle with the cheese and pour the egg mixture over.
Bake in the centre of the oven for 20 to 30 minutes or until the
mixture is well-risen and turning slightly golden on top.

To serve: For younger babies, purée to the desired texture
with an electric/hand blender, or mash/chop as required,
adding a little milk to thin down, if necessary. Serve with
bread and butter.
To store: This dish may be stored in the refrigerator for up to
24 hours or frozen for up to 1 month.

12. CHEESE DISHES

BAKED CHEESE SPECIAL
Cooking time: 25 minutes   *Calories: 165 (approx.)*

1 size 2 egg
1 tbsp natural unsweetened yoghurt
1 heaped tbsp cheddar cheese, grated

Preheat the oven to gas mark 5 (375° F/190° C). Beat all the
ingredients together lightly with a fork. Transfer to a lightly
buttered ramekin and bake in the middle of the oven for 25
minutes, or until the top is golden.

To serve: For all babies, serve as it is, hot or cold, with
tomatoes and/or bread and butter.
To store: This dish may be stored in the refrigerator for up to
24 hours, but should not be frozen.

CHEESE AND TOMATO PIZZA
Cooking time: a few minutes   *Calories: 130 (approx.)*

1 heaped tbsp cheddar cheese, grated
1 tomato, puréed as on page 82
1 slice wholemeal bread, crusts removed

Mix the cheese and tomato purée. Spread this evenly on the bread and place under a hot grill for about 2 minutes, or until the cheese has melted.

To serve: Cut into suitable-sized pieces and allow baby to finger-feed himself. For a more authentic look to the pizza, the bread base can be cut into a circle and the pizza cut into wedges when cooked!
To store: This dish should be served straightaway.

CHEESE AND CUCUMBER PURÉE
No cooking   *Calories: 130 (approx.)*

1 oz (25g) cheddar cheese, cut into small pieces
Small chunk of cucumber, peeled

Purée the cheese to the required texture with an electric blender, adding as much cucumber as necessary for the desired consistency.

To serve: Serve with bread and butter.
To store: This dish is best made as required and served straightaway.

COTTAGE LOAF
Cooking time: 25 minutes   *Calories: 210 (approx.)*

1 slice wholemeal bread, crusts removed and cut into small
   pieces
2 oz (50g) cottage cheese
1 size 2 egg

Preheat the oven to gas mark 5 (375° F/190° C). Mash all the ingredients together, place in a suitable-sized, lightly buttered, ovenproof dish and bake in the middle of the oven for 25 minutes or until the top is lightly golden and firm to the touch.

To serve: Serve hot or cold, cut into suitable-sized pieces for baby to finger-feed himself. The loaf is delicious spread very thinly with Marmite. Serve with quartered tomatoes.
To store: This loaf may be stored in the refrigerator for up to 24 hours, but should not be frozen.

CHEESE AND TOMATO PIE
Cooking time: 25 minutes   *Calories: 168 (approx.)*

1 large slice of bread, crusts removed and buttered
Enough sliced cheddar cheese to cover half of the bread
Enough slices of tomato to cover half of the bread
½ egg yolk
3 tbsp milk

Preheat the oven to gas mark 5 (375° F/190°C). Make a cheese and tomato sandwich with the first three ingredients and place in a small lightly buttered ovenproof dish. Beat the egg yolk and milk lightly with a fork and pour over the sandwich. Leave until the bread has absorbed most of the liquid, then cover the dish with foil and bake for 25 minutes in the middle of the oven.

To serve: For younger babies, mash with a fork. For older babies, roughly chop.
To store: This dish is best eaten straightaway.

BAKED CHEESE CUSTARD
Cooking time: 30 – 40 minutes   *Calories: 240 (approx.)*

6 tbsp milk
1 size 2 egg yolk
1 oz (25g) cheddar cheese, grated

Preheat the oven to gas 4 (350° F/180° C). Warm the milk, but do not boil, then remove from the heat. Beat the egg and cheese lightly with a fork then pour the warmed milk onto the egg and cheese, and mix well. Transfer to a lightly buttered ramekin, and bake in the centre of the oven for 30 to 40 minutes, or until a knife inserted halfway between the centre and side of the custard comes out clean. (If the custard is not quite cooked in the middle, the heat already present will be sufficient to finish the cooking; taking it out at this stage prevents overcooking.)

To serve: For all babies, serve as it is, hot or cold. Serve with tomatoes and bread and butter.
To store: This dish may be stored in the refrigerator for up to 24 hours, but should not be frozen.

COTTAGE PEAR
No cooking   *Calories: 140 (approx.)*

1 small ripe dessert pear
4 oz (100g) cottage cheese

For younger babies, quarter, peel and core the pear. Purée the cheese and pear until smooth with an electric/hand blender, or, sieve the cottage cheese, finely grate the pear and combine. For older babies, quarter and core the pear. Grate the flesh from the pear, discarding the skin and mix well with the cottage cheese.

To store: This dish should be eaten straightaway.

PRESSURE-COOKED CHEESY VEGETABLES

Calories: 200 (approx.)
Cooking time: 3 minutes at high pressure

1 small potato, cut into ½ inch (1cm) dice
1 small courgette, sliced
1 small carrot, sliced
1 oz (25g) cheddar cheese, grated

Pour ½ pint (285ml) of cold water into the pressure cooker. Stand the trivet rim-side down in the cooker, put the vegetables loose on the trivet and cook for 3 minutes at high pressure. Release the steam quickly.

To serve: Mash or chop the vegetables as appropriate, with the cheese (the heat from the vegetables will be sufficient to melt the cheese). Add a little cooking liquid, or milk if a thinner consistency is desired.
To store: This dish may be stored in the refrigerator for up to 24 hours or frozen for up to 1 month.

CHEESY TUNA MASH
Cooking time: 15 – 20 minutes   *Calories: 180 (approx.)*

1 smallish potato, cut into ½ inch (1cm) dice
1 heaped tbsp cheddar cheese, grated
2 oz (50g) tinned tuna, well drained
Milk

Put the potato into a suitable-sized saucepan with just enough cold water to cover it. Bring to the boil, lower the heat, cover with a fitting lid and simmer for 15 to 20 minutes or until cooked, then drain well. Mash with the cheese and tuna (the heat from the potato will be sufficient to melt the cheese) adding as much milk as necessary to achieve the desired consistency.

To serve: Serve with a green vegetable.
To store: This dish may be stored in the refrigerator for up to 24 hours or frozen for up to 1 month.

COTTAGE CHEESE SALAD 1
No cooking   *Calories: 90 (approx.)*

½ **small carrot**
1 oz (25g) tinned tuna, well drained
2 oz (50g) cottage cheese

For younger babies, slice the carrot and purée all the ingredients to the required texture with an electric blender, adding a little milk if a thinner consistency is desired. For older babies, flake the tuna, finely grate the carrot and mix well with the cottage cheese.

To store: This dish may be stored in the refrigerator for up to 24 hours, but should not be frozen.

COTTAGE CHEESE SALAD 2
No cooking   *Calories: 115 (approx.)*

1 small tomato
½ **oz (12g) cheddar cheese**
2 oz (50g) cottage cheese

For younger babies, de-skin and de-seed the tomato, cut the cheese into small pieces, then purée all the ingredients to the desired texture with an electric blender, adding a little milk if a thinner consistency is required. For older babies, grate the cheese, chop the tomato then mix all the ingredients together.

To serve: Serve with bread and butter.
To store: This dish may be stored in the refrigerator for up to 24 hours but should not be frozen.

CHEESE AND POTATO BAKE
Cooking time: 25 – 30 minutes   *Calories: 200 (approx.)*

1 small potato, cooked and mashed with a little butter
1 medium tomato, chopped
1 oz (25g) cheddar cheese, grated

Preheat the oven to gas mark 5 (375°F/190°C). Using half the ingredients put a layer of potato, tomato then cheese into a small lightly buttered ovenproof dish. Repeat with the remaining ingredients. Bake in the middle of the oven for 25 to 30 minutes.

To serve: For younger babies, mash, adding a little milk if a thinner consistency is required. Serve with green vegetables.
To store: This dish may be stored in the refrigerator for up to 24 hours or frozen for up to 1 month.

CHEDDAR SALAD 1
No cooking   *Calories: 290 (approx.)*

2 oz (50g) cheddar cheese
¼ small red pepper
1 small ripe dessert pear
Natural unsweetened yoghurt

For younger babies, purée the cheese, pepper and pear to the desired texture with an electric blender, adding a little natural yoghurt, if liked. For older babies, grate the cheese and pear, finely chop the pepper, and mix together with a little natural yoghurt.

To serve: Serve with bread and butter.
To store: This dish is best eaten straightaway.

CHEDDAR SALAD 2
No cooking   *Calories: 265 (approx.)*

2 oz (50g) cheddar cheese
2 radishes
1 large stick of celery, strings removed if prominent
2 medium tomatoes

For younger babies, slice the cheese, radishes and celery and
purée with the tomatoes to the desired texture with an electric
blender. For older babies, chop the tomatoes, grate the
cheese, radishes and celery, mix well together and serve.

To serve: Serve with bread and butter.
To store: This dish may be stored in the refrigerator for up to
24 hours or frozen for up to 1 month.

CHEDDAR FOOL
No cooking   *Calories: 160 (approx.)*

1 small dessert apple, quartered, peeled and cored
1 oz (25g) cheddar cheese

Cut the apple and cheese into small pieces and purée to the
desired texture with an electric blender, or finely grate both
and mix well together.

To store: This dish is best eaten straightaway.

13. FISH DISHES

These fish dishes may be stored in the refrigerator for up to 24 hours or frozen for up to 1 month, unless specified otherwise in the recipes.

SIMPLE SALMON SALAD
No cooking   *Calories: 70 (approx.)*

½ inch (1cm) chunk of cucumber (peeled if a very smooth purée is required)
2 oz (50g) tinned salmon, well drained
1 tbsp natural unsweetened yoghurt

Cut the cucumber into small pieces then blend all the ingredients with an electric blender to as fine or coarse a purée as necessary. Alternatively, mash the salmon, finely grate the cucumber and mix both well with the yoghurt.

To serve: Serve with bread and butter.
To store: This dish may be stored in the refrigerator for up to 24 hours, but should not be frozen.

FOIL-BAKED FISH AND TOMATO
Cooking time: 15 minutes   *Calories: 45 (approx.)*

2 oz (50g) skinned and boned white fish
1 tbsp tomato juice

Preheat the oven to gas mark 5 (375° F/190° C). Place the fish and tomato on a lightly buttered piece of foil and wrap into a parcel. Bake on a baking tray or ovenproof plate, in the middle of the oven for about 15 minutes, or until the fish flakes easily when inserted with a knife.

To serve: For younger babies, purée to the desired texture with an electric/hand blender, or mash/chop as necessary, adding a little more tomato juice if a thinner consistency is required. For older babies, cut into bite-size pieces. Serve with mixed vegetables.

JAMES'S FAVOURITE FISH BAKE
Cooking time: 20 minutes   *Calories: 110 (approx.)*

2 oz (50g) skinned and boned white fish
Tomato juice to cover the fish
1 heaped tbsp cheddar cheese, grated

Preheat the oven to gas mark 5 (375° F/190° C). Break the fish into small pieces and place in a lightly buttered ramekin. Pour over just enough tomato juice to cover the fish, sprinkle the cheese on top and bake in the centre of the oven for about 20 minutes, or until the fish is cooked.

To serve: For younger babies, purée to the desired texture with an electric/hand blender. Serve with mixed vegetables.

FISHERMAN'S PIE
Cooking time: 25 minutes   *Calories: 230 (approx.)*

**2 oz (50g) skinned and boned white fish, broken into small
    pieces**
2 tbsp milk
½ hard-boiled egg, chopped
**1 smallish potato, cooked and mashed up with a little milk
    and butter**
Small knob of butter

Preheat the oven to gas mark 6 (400° F/200° C). Put the fish
and milk into a small lightly buttered ovenproof dish, and
sprinkle egg over the top. Spread evenly with the mashed
potato and dot with the butter. Bake in the middle of the oven
for about 25 minutes, or until the top is lightly golden.

To serve: For younger babies, purée to the desired texture
with an electric/hand blender, or mash/chop as necessary,
adding a little more milk if a thinner consistency is required.
Serve with mixed vegetables.

FISH WITH CHEESY CRUMBLE TOPPING
Cooking time: 20 minutes   *Calories: 160 (approx.)*

**2 oz (50g) skinned and boned white fish, broken into small
    pieces**
2 tbsp milk
½ oz (12g) cheddar cheese
½ large slice wholemeal bread, crusts removed

Preheat the oven to gas mark 5 (375° F/190° C). Put the fish
and milk into a lightly buttered ramekin. Make the crumble
topping by cutting the cheese and bread into small pieces and
puréeing with an electric blender, or grate the bread and
cheese finely with a cheese grater and mix well. Sprinkle the
topping over the fish and bake in the middle of the oven for
about 20 minutes or until the fish is cooked.

To serve: For younger babies, purée to the desired texture with an electric/hand blender, or mash/chop as necessary, adding a little more milk if a thinner consistency is required. Serve with mixed vegetables.

FISH IN SAVOURY CUSTARD
Cooking time: 30 – 40 minutes   Calories: 215 (approx.)

2 oz (50g) skinned and boneless fish (i.e. freshly cooked white fish, or tinned and drained tuna, salmon, sardines or pilchards)
4 fl oz (142ml) milk
1 size 2 egg yolk
Tiny sprinkle of chopped parsley

Preheat the oven to gas mark 3 (325° F/170°C). Mash the fish and put into a small, lightly buttered ovenproof dish. Warm the milk, but do not boil, then remove from the heat. Beat the egg yolk and parsley lightly with a fork, then pour on the warmed milk and mix well. Pour the egg and milk mixture over the fish and bake in the centre of the oven for 30 to 40 minutes or until a knife inserted halfway between the centre and side of the custard comes out clean. (If the custard is not quite cooked in the middle, the heat already present will be sufficient to finish the cooking; removing the dish from the oven at this stage prevents overcooking.)

To serve: For younger babies, blend with an electric/hand blender, or mash/chop as necessary. Serve with bread and butter.
To store: This dish may be stored in a refrigerator for up to 24 hours but should not be frozen.

FISH FLORENTINE
Cooking time: 20 minutes   Calories: 120 (approx.)

4 – 5 spinach leaves
2 tbsp milk

Fish Florentine—contd.

2 oz (50g) skinned and boned white fish
1 heaped tbsp cheddar cheese, grated

Preheat the oven to gas mark 5 (375°F/190°C). Wash the spinach well under running cold water, then shake it to remove as much moisture as you can. Remove the centre stalk and any blemished leaves, and break into small pieces. Purée the spinach and milk with an electric blender until almost smooth, then place the mixture in a lightly buttered ramekin. Break the fish into small pieces and put on top of the spinach, sprinkle the cheese over and bake in the centre of the oven for about 20 minutes, or until the fish is cooked.

To serve: For younger babies, purée to the desired texture with an electric/hand blender or mash/chop as necessary. Serve with mashed potato.

SARDINE AND CARROT LOAF
Cooking time: 20 – 25 minutes   Calories: 195 (approx.)

1 tinned sardine, well drained
½ large slice wholemeal bread, crusts removed
1 small carrot
Tiny sprinkle of mixed herbs
1 size 2 egg, lightly beaten with a fork

Preheat the oven to gas mark 5 (375°F/190°C). Cut up the sardine, bread and carrot, then using an electric/hand blender, blend with the herbs and as much of the egg as necessary to form a fairly thick creamy consistency. Alternatively, mash the sardine, cut the bread into tiny pieces, finely grate the carrot and mix them all together with the herbs and egg as required. Turn the mixture into a lightly buttered ramekin and bake in the middle of the oven for 20 to 25 minutes, or until a knife inserted into the centre comes out clean.

To serve: For younger babies, cut up and purée to the required texture with an electric/hand blender or mash/chop as necessary, adding a little milk if a thinner consistency is desired. For older babies, cut up as required.

TUNA SALAD
No cooking   *Calories: 130 (approx.)*

1 stick of celery, strings removed if prominent
1 small carrot
2 oz (50g) tinned tuna, well drained and flaked
½ – 1 tsp tomato purée
½ hard-boiled egg shelled and chopped
Natural unsweetened yoghurt

For younger babies, slice the celery and carrot, then using an electric blender purée with the tuna, tomato purée and egg, adding as much natural yoghurt as necessary to achieve the right consistency.

For older babies, flake/mash the tuna, grate the celery and carrot, chop the egg and mix with the tomato purée and a little natural yoghurt.

To serve: Serve with bread and butter.
To store: This dish may be stored in the refrigerator for up to 24 hours, but should not be frozen.

PRESSURE-COOKED FISH DINNER
                                Calories: 115 (approx.)
Cooking time: 3 minutes at high pressure

2 oz (50g) boned and skinned white fish
Milk to cover the fish
1 small carrot, sliced
1 small potato, cut into ½ inch (1cm) dice
A few green beans, cut into small slices

Pour ½ pint (285ml) cold water into the pressure cooker, then stand the trivet, rim-side down, in the cooker. Break the fish into small pieces and place in a ramekin with just enough milk to cover it. Stand the ramekin on the trivet. Place the vegetables loosely on the trivet. Cook for 3 minutes at high pressure. Release the steam quickly.

To serve: For younger babies, purée the fish and vegetables to the desired texture with an electric/hand blender, or mash/chop as necessary, adding a little fish stock if a thinner consistency is required. For older babies, serve as it is, with a little fish stock if liked.

TEA-TIME SPECIAL
No cooking   *Calories: 180 (approx.)*

1 small cooked potato, finely diced
2 oz (50g) tinned tuna, drained and flaked
1 small salad beetroot, grated
½ size 2 egg, hard-boiled shelled and chopped
A tiny sprinkle of chopped parsley

For younger babies, mash all the ingredients together adding a little milk if a thinner consistency is required. For older babies, combine all the ingredients and serve.

To store: This dish may be stored in the refrigerator for up to 24 hours, but should not be frozen.

SAUCY FISH DINNER
Cooking time: 15 – 20 minutes   *Calories: 130 (approx.)*

1 small carrot, thinly sliced
1 small potato, cut into ½ inch (1cm) dice
½ small onion, finely chopped
Tiny piece of bay leaf (optional)
Just enough tomato juice or tomato juice and water to cover the ingredients

2 oz (50g) skinned and boned white fish
1 tbsp frozen peas
Wheatgerm (for older babies, optional)

Place the carrot, potato, onion and bay leaf (if used) into a small saucepan with the tomato juice. Bring to the boil, lower the heat, cover with a fitting lid and simmer for 15 minutes. Add the fish and peas, bring back to the boil, lower the heat, cover and simmer for a further 3 to 4 minutes, or until the fish and vegetables are cooked.

To serve: For younger babies, strain the fish and vegetables through a sieve, reserving the cooking liquid for stock. Discard the bay leaf (if used). Purée to the desired texture with an electric/hand blender, or mash/chop as appropriate, adding as much stock as necessary to achieve the right consistency.

For older babies, reduce the liquid, if necessary, by pouring off or boiling down. Thicken (if liked) the remaining stock by adding a little wheatgerm (see below) while the stock is gently simmering, stirring all the time until the sauce thickens.

To store: This dish may be stored in the refrigerator for up to 24 hours, or frozen for up to 1 month. N.B. If this dish is to be reheated after freezing, omit the wheatgerm at the cooking stage and add as required on reheating.

FISH IN PARSLEY SAUCE
Cooking time: 10 minutes   *Calories: 200 (approx.)*

2 tsp butter
4 tsp flour
4 fl oz (112ml) milk
2 oz (50g) skinned and boned white fish, cut into small pieces
A tiny sprinkle of chopped parsley

Place all the ingredients except the parsley in a small milk pan and whisk with a balloon whisk over a medium heat until the sauce bubbles and thickens. Then lower the heat and simmer very gently, uncovered, for about 7 minutes. Stir in the parsley at the end of the cooking.

To serve: For younger babies, purée to the desired texture with an electric/hand blender, or mash/chop the fish as necessary. Serve with mixed vegetables.

To store: This dish is best made as required and served straightaway.

14. MEAT DISHES

These meat dishes may be stored in the refrigerator for up to 24 hours or frozen for up to 1 month unless specified otherwise in the recipes.

LIVER AND VEGETABLES
Cooking time: 20 minutes   *Calories: 180 (approx.)*

1 small potato, cut into ½ inch (1cm) dice
1 small carrot, sliced
Marmite stock (made by dissolving ½ tsp Marmite in ½ pint/ 285ml boiling water)
1 courgette, sliced
2 oz (50g) lamb's liver, in one thin slice, if possible

Put the potato and carrot into a suitable-sized saucepan with just enough Marmite stock to cover them. Place the courgette slices on top, then carefully lay the liver on the courgette. Bring to boiling point, lower the heat, cover with a fitting lid and simmer gently for 20 minutes, or until the liver is tender and the vegetables are cooked.

To serve: For younger babies, drain the meat and vegetables through a sieve, reserving the cooking liquid for stock. Purée to the desired texture with an electric blender, or purée the meat only and mash/chop the vegetables as required, adding as much stock as necessary to achieve the right consistency. For older babies, cut up the liver and vegetables as required and serve with as much stock as liked.

CHICKEN AND RICE SPECIAL
Cooking time: 30 minutes   *Calories: 115 (approx.)*

2 oz (50g) lean chicken, cut into about 10 cubes
½ small onion, finely chopped
¼ medium green pepper, finely chopped
Just enough tomato juice to cover the ingredients
1 tbsp wholegrain rice
Tiny sprinkle of rosemary
Wheatgerm (for older babies, optional)

Place all the ingredients (except the wheatgerm) in a suitable-sized saucepan. Bring to the boil, lower the heat, cover with a fitting lid and simmer very gently for 30 minutes or until the meat and rice are cooked.

To serve: For younger babies, drain the meat, vegetables and rice through a sieve, reserving the cooking liquid for stock. Purée to the desired texture with an electric blender, or purée the meat only and mash/chop the other ingredients, adding as much stock as required and a little more milk or water if necessary to achieve the right consistency.

For older babies, reduce the stock by boiling down or pouring off. Thicken the remainder (if liked) by adding a little wheatgerm (see below) while the stock is gently simmering and stirring continuously until the sauce thickens. Cut up if necessary, and serve.

To store: This dish may be stored in the refrigerator for up to 24 hours or frozen for up to 1 month. N.B. If this dish is to be reheated after freezing, omit the wheatgerm at the cooking stage and add as required on reheating.

COLD CHICKEN OR TURKEY SALAD
No cooking   *Calories: 115 (approx.)*

2 oz (50g) cooked, lean chicken or turkey
1 small carrot
1 small stick of celery
¼ dessert apple, peeled and cored
Natural unsweetened yoghurt

For younger babies, slice the chicken, carrot, celery and apple, and purée to the desired texture with an electric blender, adding a little natural yoghurt if a thinner consistency is required. For older babies, finely chop the meat, grate the carrot, celery and apple with a cheese grater and mix well with a little natural yoghurt.

To store: This dish may be stored in the refrigerator for up to 24 hours, but should not be frozen.

PRESSURE-COOKED MEAT DINNER
                                    Calories: 160 (approx.)
Cooking time: 3 minutes at high pressure

2 oz (50g) meat, cut into ½ inch (1cm) dice. Stewing beef, veal or lamb (trimmed of all visible fat); liver; kidney (trimmed of fat, skinned and cored); chicken or turkey are all suitable. (You may also use lean, minced beef, veal or lamb, but this should be tossed and separated in its own fat in a non-stick pan over a moderate heat first, to allow the fat to run out, and then drained well on paper kitchen towel.)
Water or tomato juice to cover the meat
1 small potato, cut into ½ inch (1cm) dice
2 other vegetables of your choice, suitably prepared and cut up
Tiny sprinkle of mixed herbs (optional)

Pour ½ pint (285ml) cold water into the cooker, then stand the trivet, rim-side down, in the cooker. Place the meat and water or tomato juice in a ramekin and stand it on the trivet. Place the vegetables in little piles directly on the trivet and sprinkle with herbs, if used. Cook for 3 minutes at high pressure. Release the steam quickly.

To serve: For younger babies, drain the meat through a sieve, reserving the liquid for stock. Purée with the vegetables to the desired texture using an electric blender, or purée the meat only and mash/chop the vegetables as required, adding as much meat stock and/or cooking water as necessary to achieve the right consistency. For older babies, cut up, if necessary, and serve with a little meat stock, if liked.

BEEF STEW
Cooking time: 1½ hours   *Calories: 160 (approx.)*

2 oz (50g) chuck steak, trimmed of all visible fat and cut into
   about 10 cubes
1 small carrot, sliced
1 small potato, cut into ½ inch (1cm) dice
½ small onion, chopped
1 tsp pot barley
Just enough water to cover the ingredients

Place all the ingredients in a suitable-sized saucepan. Bring to the boil, lower the heat, cover with a fitting lid and simmer very gently for 1½ hours, or until the meat is tender.

To serve: As for Liver and Vegetables, page 140, for younger babies. For older babies, reduce the stock if necessary by boiling down or pouring off. Cut up, if required, and serve.

LIVER PÂTÉ
No cooking　　　　　　　　　*Calories: 140 (approx.)*

About 2 oz (50g) lamb's liver, cooked and finely puréed
Cottage cheese, sieved
Level tsp tomato purée (optional)

Mix the liver with enough cottage cheese and tomato purée (if used) to form a spreadable mixture.

To serve: For younger babies, thin down with a little milk or water and spoon-feed to baby. For older babies, serve on bread or toast, and cut into suitable-sized pieces for baby to feed himself.
To store: This dish may be stored in the refrigerator for up to 24 hours, but should not be frozen.

GOULASH
Cooking time: 2 hours　　　　　*Calories: 95 (approx.)*

2 oz (50g) chuck steak, trimmed of all visible fat and cut into
　　about 12 cubes
Olive oil
½ small onion, chopped
Slice of green pepper, finely chopped
Equal quantities of tomato juice and water, just enough to
　　cover the ingredients
Wheatgerm (for older babies, optional)
Natural unsweetened yoghurt (for older babies, optional)

Brown the meat lightly in the oil and drain well. Place in a suitable-sized saucepan with the rest of the ingredients, except the yoghurt and wheatgerm. Bring to the boil, lower the heat, cover with a fitting lid and simmer very gently for 1½ hours or until the meat is tender.

To serve: For younger babies, drain the meat and vegetables

through a sieve, reserving the cooking liquid for stock. Purée
to the desired texture with an electric blender, or purée the
meat only and mash/chop the vegetables as required, adding
as much stock as necessary to achieve the right consistency.

For older babies, reduce the stock if necessary by boiling
down or pouring off. Thicken the remainder (if liked) by
adding a little wheatgerm (see below) while the stock is gently
simmering, stirring continuously until the sauce thickens.
Remove from the heat, stir in a little natural yoghurt (if
liked), cut up if necessary and serve.

Serve with mashed potato or rice.

To store: This dish may be stored in the refrigerator for up to
24 hours, or frozen for up to 1 month. N.B. If this dish is to be
reheated after freezing, omit the wheatgerm and yoghurt at
the cooking stage and add as required on reheating.

KIDNEY STEW
Cooking time: 20 minutes   *Calories: 130 (approx.)*

2 lamb's kidneys, cores snipped out with a pair of scissors
1 small carrot, sliced
½ small onion, finely chopped
Just enough Marmite stock to cover the ingredients (made by
   dissolving ½ tsp Marmite in ½ pint/285ml boiling water)

Place all the ingredients in a suitable-sized saucepan. Bring
up to the boil, lower the heat, cover with a fitting lid and
simmer for 20 minutes, or until the kidneys are tender.

To serve: As for Liver and Vegetables, page 140, for younger
babies. For older babies, serve with as much stock as liked.
Serve with potatoes.

BEEF HOTPOT
Cooking time: 2 hours   *Calories: 145 (approx.)*

2 oz (50g) chuck steak, cut into about 10 cubes
Olive oil
1 small potato, cut into ½ inch (1cm) dice
1 small carrot, sliced
1 stick of celery, chopped
3 tbsp Marmite stock (made by dissolving a dot of Marmite in
   3 tbsp of water which has just boiled)

Preheat the oven to gas mark 2 (300° F/150° C). Brown the
meat lightly in the oil then drain well. Place in a small
ovenproof dish with the rest of the ingredients, cover with
foil, tie up with string and bake in the middle of the oven for 2
hours, or until the meat is tender and the vegetables are
cooked.

To serve: For younger babies, purée all the ingredients to the
desired texture with an electric blender, or purée the meat
only and mash/chop the vegetables as necessary, adding a
little milk or water if a thinner consistency is required. For
older babies, cut up as required and serve.

MINCE AND PARSNIP BAKE
Cooking time: 1 hour   *Calories: 90 (approx.)*

2 oz (50g) lean minced beef
1 parsnip, coarsely grated
3 tbsp water
Tiny sprinkle of mixed herbs

Preheat the oven to gas mark 5 (375° F/190° C). Toss and
separate the meat in a non-stick pan in its own fat over a
moderate heat until the fat runs out and the meat is lightly
browned, but still soft. Then drain well on paper kitchen
towel. Mix well with the other ingredients and place in a

small, lightly buttered, ovenproof dish. Cover with foil, tie up with string and bake towards the top of the oven for 1 hour, or until the meat is tender and the vegetables are cooked.

To serve: As for Beef Hotpot, page 145, with a green vegetable.

SHEPHERD'S PIE
Cooking time: 40 minutes   *Calories: 250 (approx.)*

1 smallish potato, cut into ½ inch (1cm) dice
2 oz (50g) cold cooked lean meat
2 tbsp tomato juice
1 heaped tbsp cheddar cheese, grated
Milk
Knob of butter

Preheat the oven to gas mark 5 (375°F/190°C). Put the potato into a suitable-sized saucepan with just enough cold water to cover it. Bring to the boil, lower the heat, cover with a fitting lid and simmer for 15 minutes, or until the potato is cooked, then drain. Meanwhile, for younger babies, purée the meat and tomato juice together with an electric blender to the desired texture; for older babies, chop the meat finely and mix with the tomato juice. Place the mixture in a lightly buttered, small ovenproof dish. When the potato is ready, mash with the cheese, adding as much milk and butter as necessary to achieve a smooth creamy consistency. Spread evenly over the meat mixture and bake in the middle of the oven for 20 to 25 minutes, or until lightly golden on top.

To serve: For younger babies, mash and thin down if necessary, with a little milk or water. Serve with mixed vegetables.

CHICKEN AND APRICOTS
Cooking time: 20 minutes   *Calories: 125 (approx.)*

2 oz (50g) cooked lean chicken
4 moisturised and ready-to-eat dried apricots
Milk

Preheat the oven to gas mark 6 (400° F/200° C). Purée the
chicken and apricots to the desired texture with an electric
blender, adding as much milk as necessary to achieve the
right consistency. Place in a lightly buttered ramekin, cover
with foil, tie up with string and bake in the middle of the oven
for 20 minutes.

To serve: Serve with bread and butter or mixed vegetables.

LIVER AND SWEDE SPECIAL
Cooking time: 20 minutes   *Calories: 210 (approx.)*

1 very small swede, cut into ½ inch (1cm) dice
2 oz (50g) lamb's liver in one thin slice, if possible
1 heaped tbsp cheddar cheese, grated

Place the swede in a suitable-sized saucepan with just enough
cold water to cover it, then lay the liver carefully on top of the
swede. Bring to the boil, lower the heat, cover with a fitting lid
and simmer for 20 minutes, or until the swede is cooked and
the liver is tender.

To serve: For younger babies, drain the meat and swede
through a sieve, reserving the cooking liquid for stock. Purée
the liver, swede and cheese to the desired texture with an
electric blender, adding as much cooking liquid as necessary
to achieve the right consistency. For older babies, cut up the
liver as required. Mash the swede with the cheese and a little
cooking liquid and serve.

LIVER AND ONION CASSEROLE
Cooking time: 45 minutes   *Calories: 110 (approx.)*

2 oz (50g) lamb's liver, in one thin slice if possible
½ small onion, finely chopped
Just enough Marmite stock to cover the ingredients (made by
** dissolving ½ level tsp Marmite in ½ pint/285ml boiling**
** water)**

Preheat the oven to gas mark 5 (375° F/190° C). Cut the liver
into 2 or 3 pieces and place in a lightly buttered ramekin,
sprinkle the onion over the top, pour over the stock and bake
in the middle of the oven for 45 minutes, or until the liver is
tender.

To serve: For younger babies, drain the meat and onion
through a sieve, reserving the cooking liquid for stock. Purée
to the desired texture with an electric blender, or chop up the
meat, as appropriate, adding as much stock as necessary to
achieve the right consistency. For older babies, cut up the
meat as required. Serve with mixed vegetables.

BAKED LIVER LOAF
Cooking time: 20 – 25 minutes   ·   *Calories: 230 (approx.)*

2 oz (50g) lamb's liver
½ large slice wholemeal bread, crusts removed
½ small onion, chopped
1 size 2 egg, lightly beaten with a fork

Preheat the oven to gas mark 5 (375° F/190° C). Cut up the
liver and bread. Using an electric blender, blend with the
onion and as much of the egg as necessary to form a fairly
thick creamy consistency. Turn the mixture into a lightly
buttered ramekin and bake in the middle of the oven for 20 to
25 minutes, or until a knife comes out clean when inserted
into the centre.

To serve: For younger babies, cut up and purée to the desired texture with an electric/hand blender, adding a little milk to achieve a thinner consistency if required. For older babies, mash or chop as necessary. Goes well with mixed vegetables or tomatoes.

CHICKEN CASSEROLE
Cooking time: 1 hour   *Calories: 140 (approx.)*

½ **rasher of back bacon, trimmed of all fat and chopped**
Olive oil
2 oz (50g) lean chicken, cut into about 10 cubes
1 small carrot, sliced
½ **small onion, chopped**
½ **small turnip, cut into** ½ **inch (1cm) dice**
Tiny sprinkle of thyme
3 tbsp water

Preheat the oven to gas mark 6 (400°F/200°C). Fry the bacon in the hot oil for a minute or two then drain well. Mix with the other ingredients, place in a small, lightly buttered ovenproof dish, cover with foil, tie up with string, and bake in the middle of the oven for 1 hour, or until the meat is tender.

To serve: For younger babies, purée all the ingredients to the desired texture with an electric blender, or purée the meat only and mash/chop the vegetables as necessary, adding a little previously boiled milk or water if a thinner consistency is required. For older babies, cut up as required and serve.

LAMB AND BEAN STEW
Cooking time: 20 minutes   *Calories: 140 (approx.)*

2 oz (50g) lean minced lamb
2 tbsp cooked haricot beans (see page 83), or tinned baked
   beans

½ small onion, grated
1 small stick of celery, chopped
Just enough tomato juice or tomato juice and water to cover
   the ingredients
Wheatgerm (for older babies, optional)

Toss and separate the lamb in a non-stick saucepan in its own
fat over a moderate heat, until the meat is lightly browned
and all the fat has run out, then drain well on paper kitchen
towel. Return the meat to the pan with the rest of the
ingredients, except the wheatgerm. Bring to the boil, lower
the heat, cover with a fitting lid and simmer for 20 minutes.

To serve and to store: As for Goulash, page 143, without
adding the yoghurt.

FOIL-BAKED KIDNEY AND TOMATO
Cooking time: 30 minutes   *Calories: 60 (approx.)*

1 lamb's kidney, fat, skin and core removed and sliced
2 tbsp tomato juice

Preheat the oven to gas mark 5 (375° F/190° C). Wrap the
kidney and tomato juice securely in lightly buttered
aluminium foil and bake on a tray in the middle of the oven
for about 30 minutes, or until the kidney is tender.

To serve: For younger babies, purée the contents of the foil
with an electric blender, or chop finely, adding a little extra
tomato juice or previously boiled water if a thinner
consistency is required. For older babies, cut up the kidney as
required and serve with the cooking liquid poured over. Serve
with mixed vegetables.

15. VEGETABLE DISHES

These vegetable dishes may be stored in the refrigerator for up to 24 hours or frozen for up to 1 month, unless specified otherwise in the recipes.

SUMMER VEGETABLE CASSEROLE
Cooking time: 15 – 20 minutes   Calories: 85 (approx.)

1 small potato, cut into ½ inch (1cm) dice
1 small carrot, sliced
3 green beans, cut into ½ inch (1cm) lengthways slices
1 tbsp frozen sweetcorn
Just enough tomato juice or tomato juice and water to cover the ingredients
Wheatgerm (for older babies, optional)

Put all the ingredients except the wheatgerm into a suitable-sized saucepan. Bring just to the boil, lower the heat, cover with a fitting lid and simmer for 15 to 20 minutes, or until all the vegetables are cooked.

To serve: For younger babies, strain the vegetables through a sieve, reserving the cooking liquid for stock. Purée to the desired texture with an electric/hand blender, or mash/chop as necessary, adding as much stock as needed to achieve the right consistency.

For older babies, reduce the liquid if necessary, by boiling down or pouring off. Thicken the remainder (if liked) by adding a little wheatgerm (see below) while the stock is gently simmering, stirring continously until the sauce thickens.

To store: This dish may be stored in the refrigerator for up to 24 hours or frozen for up to 1 month. N.B. If this dish is to be reheated after freezing, omit the wheatgerm at the cooking stage and add as required on reheating.

CAULIFLOWER WITH CHEESE SAUCE
Cooking time: 20 minutes　　　　*Calories: 240 (approx.)*

A few sprigs of cauliflower
2 tsp butter
4 tsp flour
4 fl oz (112ml) milk
1 heaped tbsp cheddar cheese, grated

Place the cauliflower in a suitable-sized saucepan with just enough cold water to cover it. Bring to the boil, lower the heat, cover with a fitting lid and simmer for 5 to 10 minutes, or until almost cooked. Drain through a sieve, reserving the cooking liquid and keep warm. Place the butter, flour and milk in the same saucepan and whisk with a balloon whisk over a medium heat until the sauce bubbles and thickens. Then add the cauliflower, lower the heat and simmer very gently, uncovered, for about 7 minutes. Add the cheese, stirring continuously until it melts, then serve.

To serve: For younger babies, purée to the desired texture with an electric/hand blender, adding a little of the cooking liquid if a thinner consistency is required. For older babies, cut up the cauliflower as required and serve as it is with meat

or other vegetables if baby's appetite demands it.
To store: This dish is best eaten straightaway.

MILKY POTATOES WITH CHEESE
Cooking time: 15 – 20 minutes   Calories: 170 (approx.)

1 small potato, cut into ½ inch (1cm) dice
Just enough milk to cover the potato
1 heaped tbsp cheddar cheese, grated

Place the potato and milk into a suitable-sized saucepan,
bring just to simmering point, lower the heat and continue to
simmer, uncovered, for 15 minutes, or until the potato is
cooked.

To serve: Drain the potato through a sieve, reserving the
milk. With a fork, mash with the cheese until smooth (the
heat from the potato will be sufficient to melt the cheese)
and add as much of the milk as necessary to achieve the right
consistency.

SPEEDY BEANY
Cooking time: a few minutes   Calories: 190 (approx.)

3 rounded tbsp baked beans
1 heaped tbsp cheddar cheese, grated
**1 large slice wholemeal bread, crusts removed and cut into
  ½ inch (1cm) squares**

Place all the ingredients in a suitable-sized saucepan and
warm without boiling over a gentle heat for a few minutes, or
until the cheese has melted, stirring continuously.

To serve: For younger babies, mash finely with a fork, adding
a little previously boiled milk or water if a thinner consistency
is required. For older babies, serve as it is, or thin down a little
with milk first if necessary.

MIXED ROOT MASH
Cooking time: 20 minutes   *Calories: 120 (approx.)*

1 small potato, cut into ½ inch (1cm) dice
1 small parsnip, sliced
Butter

Place the potato and parsnip in a suitable-sized saucepan with just enough cold water to cover them. Bring to the boil, lower the heat, cover with a fitting lid and simmer for 15 minutes, or until cooked.

To serve: Drain the vegetables through a sieve, reserving the cooking liquid. Mash until smooth with a little butter, adding as much cooking liquid as necessary to achieve the desired consistency.

STUFFED BAKED POTATO
Cooking time: 55 minutes   *Calories: 180 (approx.)*

1 smallish potato, scrubbed but not peeled, with a small slit
  cut in the top
1 heaped tbsp cheddar cheese, grated
Milk
Butter

Preheat the oven to gas mark 6 (400° F/200° C). Bake the potato in the middle of the oven for about 45 minutes, or until cooked. Slice in half, scoop out potato and mash to a creamy consistency with the cheese and a little milk and butter. Put the filling back into the jackets and return to the oven for 10 minutes or so, to heat through again, if desired. Otherwise serve to baby as it is, or cut up as required for him to feed himself.

LENTIL SUPREME
Cooking time: 30 minutes   *Calories: 160 (approx.)*

3 rounded tbsp red lentils
Tomato juice to cover the lentils
1 heaped tbsp cheddar cheese, grated

Place the lentils and tomato juice in a suitable-sized saucepan. Bring just to boiling point, lower the heat, cover with a fitting lid and simmer for 30 minutes or until the lentils are tender, adding a little more tomato juice during cooking if necessary.

To serve: For younger babies, drain the lentils through a sieve, reserving the cooking liquid. Mash to the desired texture with the cheese (the heat from the lentils will be sufficient to melt the cheese), adding as much cooking liquid as necessary to achieve the right consistency. For older babies, reduce the liquid by boiling down or pouring off, then add the cheese, stirring continuously until it melts, and serve.

WINTER VEGETABLE CASSEROLE
Cooking time: 15 – 20 minutes   *Calories: 90 (approx.)*

1 small potato, cut into ½ inch (1cm) dice
Slice of swede, cut into ½ inch (1cm) dice
3 small sprouts
1 tbsp frozen peas
Just enough Marmite stock to cover the ingredients (made by dissolving ½ tsp Marmite in ½ pint/285ml boiling water)
Wheatgerm (for older babies, optional)

Put all the ingredients except the wheatgerm into a suitable-sized saucepan. Bring to the boil, lower the heat, cover with a fitting lid and simmer for 15 to 20 minutes, or until all the vegetables are cooked.

To serve and to store: As for Summer Vegetable Casserole, page 151.

COURGETTE WITH CHEESE AND TOMATO
Cooking time: 10 – 15 minutes   *Calories: 80 (approx.)*

1 small courgette, sliced
1 heaped tbsp cheddar cheese, grated
Tomato juice

Place the courgette in a suitable-sized saucepan with just enough cold water to cover it. Bring to the boil, lower the heat, cover with a fitting lid and simmer for 10 minutes or until cooked, then drain.

To serve: For younger babies, purée the courgette and cheese to the desired texture with an electric/hand blender or mash with a fork (the heat from the courgette will be sufficient to melt the cheese), adding a little tomato juice to taste. For older babies, roughly chop the courgette with the cheese, so that the cheese melts, then stir in a little tomato juice to taste.
To store: This dish is best eaten straightaway.

CARROT SPECIAL
Cooking time: 20 minutes   *Calories: 90 (approx.)*

2 small carrots, sliced
1 heaped tbsp cheddar cheese, grated
Natural unsweetened yoghurt

Place the carrots in a suitable-sized saucepan with just enough cold water to cover them. Bring to the boil, cover with a fitting lid and simmer for 8 minutes or until tender, then drain.

To serve: For younger babies, mash the carrots with the cheese (the heat from the carrots will be sufficient to melt the cheese) adding as much natural yoghurt as required to achieve the right consistency. For older babies, mash the carrots with most of the cheese and a little natural yoghurt.

Place in a small, lightly buttered ovenproof dish, sprinkle the rest of the cheese over the top and brown under a hot grill.
To store: This dish is best eaten straightaway.

RATATOUILLE
Cooking time: 10 minutes   *Calories: 50 (approx.)*

½ small onion, finely grated
Small chunk (about 2 oz/50g) aubergine, cut into ½ inch (1cm) dice
1 small courgette, cut into quarters lengthways, then sliced
A small chunk of red pepper, finely chopped
Just enough tomato juice or tomato juice and water to cover the ingredients

Put all the ingredients into a suitable-sized saucepan. Bring just to the boil, lower the heat, cover with a fitting lid and simmer for about 10 minutes, or until all the vegetables are cooked.

To serve: As for Summer Vegetable Casserole, page 151, without adding the wheatgerm for older babies.

AVOCADO SAVOURY
No cooking   *Calories: 300 (approx.)*

½ ripe avocado pear
1 rounded tbsp natural unsweetened yoghurt
1 heaped tbsp cheddar cheese, grated

Scoop out the flesh from the avocado pear and mash until smooth with the yoghurt and cheese, adding a little milk if a thinner consistency is required.
To store: This dish is best eaten straightaway.

MIXED VEGETABLE BAKE WITH OPTIONAL CRUMBLE TOPPING

Cooking time: 1 hour   *Calories: 110 (approx.)*

1 medium tomato, chopped
1 small potato, finely diced
1 carrot, finely chopped
½ small onion, grated
1 tbsp frozen sweetcorn
1 tbsp frozen peas
2 tbsp water
Tiny sprinkle of mixed herbs

For the topping
½ large slice wholemeal bread
½ oz (12g) cheddar cheese

Preheat the oven to gas mark 5 (375°F/190°C). Place all the ingredients, except those for the topping, in a suitable-sized lightly buttered ovenproof dish. Cover with foil, tie it with string and bake in the middle of the oven for 45 minutes, or until all the vegetables are cooked. Meanwhile, make the topping by cutting the bread and cheese into small pieces and puréeing them to a crumbly texture with an electric blender. Remove the foil from the vegetable bake, sprinkle the topping over it and return to the oven for a further 15 minutes, or until golden on top.

To serve: For younger babies, purée to the desired texture with an electric/hand blender, adding a little milk or water if a thinner consistency is required. For older babies, serve as it is.

CARROT AND PARSLEY CREAM
Cooking time: 7 minutes   *Calories: 180 (approx.)*

2 tsp butter
4 tsp flour
4 fl oz (112ml) milk
2 medium carrots, finely grated
Sprinkle of parsley

Place all the ingredients in a small, preferably non-stick, milk pan. Whisk with a balloon whisk over a medium heat until the sauce bubbles and thickens, then reduce the heat and simmer very gently, uncovered, for 7 minutes.

To serve: For younger babies, thin down with a little milk if a thinner consistency is required. For older babies, serve as it is.
To store: This dish is best served straightaway.

16. RICE AND PASTA DISHES

CHEESY RICEBURGERS
Cooking time: 5 minutes   *Calories: 450 (approx.)*

2 tbsp wholegrain rice, cooked
1 small carrot, finely grated
2 heaped tbsp cheddar cheese, grated
Egg, beaten

Combine the rice, carrot and cheese with a little egg to bind
the ingredients together. Shape the mass into about 4
burgers. Remove mesh from grillpan and cook under a
preheated hot grill for 2 to 3 minutes on each side, or until
slightly golden.

To serve: Cut into suitable-sized pieces and allow baby to
finger-feed himself.
To store: This dish is best eaten freshly made.

SALMON KEDGEREE
Cooking time: 30 minutes   *Calories: 225 (approx.)*

2 tbsp wholegrain rice
2 oz (50g) tinned or freshly cooked salmon, mashed
1 size 2 egg, hard-boiled, shelled and chopped

Place the rice with 4 tbsp of cold water in a suitable-sized saucepan. Bring to the boil, lower the heat, cover with a fitting lid and simmer gently until all the liquid has been absorbed and the rice is tender (about 30 minutes).

To serve: For younger babies, purée all the ingredients with an electric/hand blender, or mash/chop as necessary, adding a little milk if a thinner consistency is required. For older babies, mix all the ingredients together and serve as it is.
To store: This dish may be stored in the refrigerator for up to 24 hours, but should not be frozen.

TOMATO RICE WITH CHEESE
Cooking time: 35 minutes   *Calories: 200 (approx.)*

2 tbsp wholegrain rice
4 tbsp tomato juice
1 oz (25g) cheddar cheese, grated

Place the rice and tomato juice in a suitable-sized saucepan. Bring to the boil, lower the heat, cover with a fitting lid and simmer gently until all the liquid has been absorbed and the rice is cooked. Add the cheese, stirring continuously until it melts.

To serve: For younger babies, purée to the desired texture with an electric/hand blender, or by pushing through a sieve with the back of a spoon, adding a little more tomato juice, or water if a thinner consistency is required. For older babies, serve as it is.
To store: This dish may be stored in the refrigerator for up to 24 hours, or frozen for up to 1 month.

MACARONI CHEESE
Cooking time: 12 minutes   *Calories: 330 (approx.)*

2 rounded tbsp wholewheat short-cut macaroni
2 tsp butter
4 tsp flour
4 fl oz (112ml) milk
1 oz (25g) cheddar cheese, grated

Put the macaroni into a suitable-sized saucepan. Cover with
plenty of cold water. Bring to the boil, lower the heat, cover
with a fitting lid and simmer gently for about 12 minutes, or
until cooked, then drain. Meanwhile, put the butter, flour
and milk into a small, preferably non-stick, milk pan and
whisk with a balloon whisk over a medium heat until the
sauce bubbles and thickens. Lower the heat and simmer very
gently, uncovered, for about 7 minutes. Add the macaroni
and cheese, stirring continuously until the cheese melts, then
serve.

To serve: For younger babies, purée to the desired texture
with an electric/hand blender, or by pushing through a sieve
with the back of a spoon, adding a little milk or water if a
thinner consistency is required. For older babies, serve as it is.
To store: This dish is best eaten straightaway.

SPAGHETTI BOLOGNESE
Cooking time: 20 minutes   *Calories: 230 (approx.)*

2 oz (50g) lean minced beef
½ small onion, grated
Tiny sprinkle of mixed herbs
Just enough tomato juice or tomato juice and water to cover
**   the ingredients**
Wholewheat spaghetti, broken into ½ inch (1cm) lengths
Wheatgerm (for older babies, optional)
A little cheddar or Parmesan cheese, grated (optional)

Using a suitable-sized saucepan, toss and separate the meat in its own fat, over a moderate heat, until the fat runs out and the meat is lightly browned, but still soft, then drain well on paper kitchen towel. Return the meat to the pan with the onion, herbs and liquid. Bring just to the boil, lower the heat, cover with a fitting lid and simmer for 20 minutes.

To cook the spaghetti, put the amount required into a suitable-sized saucepan containing plenty of boiling water. Bring back to the boil, lower the heat, cover with a fitting lid and simmer gently for about 12 minutes, or until cooked, then drain well.

To serve: For younger babies, strain the sauce through a sieve, reserving the cooking liquid. Purée the sauce and spaghetti to the desired texture with an electric/hand blender, or purée the sauce only and mash/chop the spaghetti as required, adding as much cooking liquid as necessary to achieve the right consistency.

For older babies, reduce the sauce, if necessary, by boiling down or pouring off. Thicken the remainder (if liked) by adding a little wheatgerm (see below) while the sauce is gently simmering, stirring continuously until it thickens. Serve with the spaghetti and sprinkled with a little grated cheddar or Parmesan cheese, if desired.

To store: As for Mock Lamb Curry with Rice, page 165.

BEEF, BEANS AND PASTA
Cooking time: 20 minutes   *Calories: 220 (approx.)*

2 oz (50g) lean minced beef
1 well-rounded tbsp baked beans
½ small onion, grated
1 oz (25g) wholewheat pasta shapes
Tomato juice to cover the ingredients
Wheatgerm (for older babies, optional)

Using a suitable-sized non-stick saucepan, toss and separate the meat in its own fat over a moderate heat, until lightly browned, but still soft, then drain well on paper kitchen towel. Return the meat to the pan with the other ingredients (except the wheatgerm), bring to the boil, lower the heat, cover with a fitting lid and simmer for 20 minutes.

To serve: For younger babies, strain the ingredients through a sieve, reserving the cooking liquid. Purée to the desired texture with an electric/hand blender, or mash/chop as required, adding as much cooking liquid as necessary to achieve the right consistency.

For older babies, reduce the liquid if necessary, by boiling down or pouring off. Thicken any remainder (if liked) by adding a little wheatgerm (see below) while the sauce is gently simmering, stirring continuously until it thickens.

To store: This dish may be stored in the refrigerator for up to 24 hours, or frozen for up to 1 month. N.B. If the sauce is to be reheated after freezing, omit the wheatgerm at the cooking stage and add as required on reheating.

MOCK LAMB CURRY WITH RICE
Cooking time: 35 minutes   *Calories: 190 (approx.)*

2 tbsp wholegrain rice
2 oz (50g) lean minced lamb
½ small onion, grated
1 tsp lemon juice
1 tsp mango chutney
Tiny sprinkle of medium-hot curry powder
Just enough tomato juice or tomato juice and water to cover
   the ingredients
Wheatgerm (for older babies, optional)

Place the rice with 4 tbsp of cold water in a suitable-sized saucepan. Bring to the boil, lower the heat, cover with a fitting lid and simmer gently until all the liquid has been absorbed and the rice is tender (about 30 minutes).

To make the sauce: Using a suitable-sized non-stick saucepan, toss and separate the meat in its own fat over a moderate heat until the fat runs out and the meat is lightly browned but still soft, then drain well on paper kitchen towel. Return the meat to the pan with the rest of the ingredients (except the rice and wheatgerm). Bring just to the boil, lower the heat, cover with a fitting lid and simmer for 20 minutes.

To serve: For younger babies, strain the sauce through a sieve, reserving the cooking liquid. Purée the sauce and rice to the desired texture with an electric/hand blender, or purée the sauce only, adding as much cooking liquid as necessary to achieve the right consistency.

For older babies, reduce the sauce, if necessary, by boiling down or-pouring off. Thicken the remainder (if liked) by adding a little wheatgerm (see below) while the sauce is gently simmering, stirring continuously until it thickens. Serve with the rice.

To store: The sauce alone or the sauce and rice combined in a purée may be stored in the refrigerator for up to 24 hours or frozen for up to 1 month. If the rice is to be served as an accompaniment to the sauce, it is best freshly made as required. N.B. If the sauce is to be reheated after freezing, omit the wheatgerm at the cooking stage and add as required on reheating.

MOCK CHILLI CON CARNE WITH RICE
Cooking time: 35 minutes   *Calories: 190 (approx.)*

2 tbsp wholegrain rice
2 oz (50g) lean minced beef
½ small onion, grated
Slice of green pepper, finely chopped
Tiny sprinkle of chilli powder
1 tbsp cooked (see Dried Bean Purée recipe, page 83) or tinned red kidney beans

Mock Chilli Con Carne With Rice—contd.

Just enough stock (½ water, ½ tomato juice) to cover the ingredients
Wheatgerm (for older babies, optional)

Place the rice with 4 tbsp of cold water in a suitable-sized saucepan. Bring to the boil, lower the heat, cover with a fitting lid and simmer gently until all the liquid has been absorbed and the rice is tender (about 30 minutes).

To make the sauce: Using a suitable-sized non-stick saucepan, toss and separate the meat in its own fat over a moderate heat until the fat runs out and the meat is lightly browned but still soft, then drain well on paper kitchen towel. Return the meat to the pan with the rest of the ingredients (except the rice and wheatgerm). Bring just to the boil, lower the heat, cover with a fitting lid and simmer for 20 minutes.

To serve and to store: As for Mock Lamb Curry with Rice, page 165.

EGG AND TUNA SPAGHETTI
Cooking time: 15 minutes　　　　　*Calories: 240 (approx.)*

1 oz (25g) wholewheat spaghetti
1 oz (25g) tinned tuna, well drained and flaked
½ size 2 egg, lightly beaten
1 heaped tbsp cheddar cheese, grated

To cook the spaghetti, put the required amount into a suitable-sized saucepan containing plenty of boiling water. Bring back to the boil, lower the heat, cover with a fitting lid and simmer gently for about 12 minutes, or until cooked, then drain well. Return to the pan with the remaining ingredients and cook for a minute or two, stirring all the time, until the cheese melts and the egg begins to thicken.

To serve: For younger babies, purée to the desired texture

with an electric blender, or mash/chop as necessary, adding a little milk or water if a thinner consistency is required. For older babies, cut up the spaghetti as required and serve.
To store: This dish is best freshly made as required.

SPECIAL RISOTTO
Cooking time: 30 minutes   *Calories: 210 (approx.)*

Knob of butter
½ small onion, finely chopped
2 tbsp wholegrain rice
4 tbsp Marmite stock (made by dissolving a dot of Marmite in 4 tbsp of boiling water)
1 heaped tbsp cheddar cheese, grated

Melt the butter in a suitable-sized saucepan and gently fry the onion for a few minutes. Add the rice and coat it in the butter, then pour over the stock, bring to the boil, lower the heat, cover with a fitting lid and simmer for 30 minutes, or until the rice is cooked and all the liquid has been absorbed. Add the cheese, stirring continuously until it melts, then serve.

To serve: As for Macaroni Cheese, page 162.
To store: This dish may be stored in the refrigerator for up to 24 hours or frozen for up to 1 month.

17. DELICIOUS DESSERTS

FRESH PEAR YOGHURT
No cooking   *Calories: 70 (approx.)*

1 small ripe dessert pear
2 rounded tbsp natural unsweetened yoghurt

Quarter and core the pear, then grate the flesh on the finest
section of a cheese grater, discarding the skin as you do so.
Mix with the yoghurt and serve.
To store: This dish is best freshly made as required.

BAKED EGG CUSTARD
Cooking time: 30 – 40 minutes   *Calories: 260 (approx.)*

7 fl oz (200ml) milk
1 size 2 egg
1 rounded tsp runny honey
A little nutmeg

Preheat the oven to gas mark 3 (325° F/170° C). Warm the

milk, but do not boil, then remove from the heat. Beat the egg and honey lightly with a fork, then pour on the warmed milk and mix well. Transfer into 2 lightly buttered ramekins, sprinkle with grated nutmeg and bake in the centre of the oven for 30 to 40 minutes, or until a knife inserted halfway between the centre and the side of the custard comes out clean. (If the custard is not quite cooked in the middle, the heat already present will be sufficient to finish the cooking; taking it out at this stage prevents overcooking.)

To serve: For all babies, serve as it is, hot or cold.

To store: This dish may be stored in the refrigerator for up to 24 hours, but should not be frozen.

SHARON FRUIT DELIGHT

Sharon fruits are imported from Israel and widely available in supermarkets. They look like waxy tomatoes with orange skin and flesh. When ripe, they yield to gentle pressure.

No cooking   *Calories: 150 (approx.)*

1 small sharon fruit
4 oz (100g) cottage cheese

Quarter the sharon fruit and scoop out its flesh, discarding the skin. Purée to a smooth texture with the cottage cheese, using an electric/hand blender.

To serve: For all babies, serve as it is.

To store: This dish is best freshly made as required.

APPLE FOOL
No cooking   *Calories: 70 (approx.)*

1 dessert apple, peeled, quartered, cored and cut up
1 heaped tbsp vanilla ice-cream

Purée the apple and ice-cream with an electric blender until smooth.

To serve: For all babies, serve as it is.

To store: This dish is best freshly made as required.

BLACK CHERRY CHEESECAKE
No cooking   *Calories: 200 (approx.)*

1 wholemeal shortbread finger biscuit, crushed
3 oz (75g) cottage cheese, sieved
1 heaped tsp 'no added sugar' black cherry jam

Press the biscuit crumbs into the bottom of a ramekin, spread the cottage cheese on the top, then a layer of jam.
To serve: Serve as it is.
To store: This dish may be stored in the refrigerator for up to 24 hours, but should not be frozen.

FIFTEEN-MINUTE RICE PUDDING
Cooking time: 15 minutes   *Calories: 195 (approx.)*

2 heaped tsp whole rice flakes
5 fl oz (142ml) milk
Small knob of butter
A little runny honey

Put the rice, milk and butter into a small (preferably non-stick) milk pan and bring just up to simmering point. Reduce the heat and simmer very gently, uncovered, stirring frequently, until the pudding is tender, thick and creamy. Remove from the heat and stir in a little honey to taste.

To serve: Serve hot or cold. For younger babies, purée to the desired texture with an electric/hand blender first if absolutely necessary.
To store: This dish may be stored in the refrigerator for up to 24 hours, but should not be frozen.

PLUM AND RASPBERRY CRUMBLE
Cooking time: 25 – 30 minutes   *Calories: 200 (approx.)*

1 dessert plum
1 well-rounded tsp 'no added sugar' raspberry jam

For the topping
Small knob of butter
2 tbsp wholemeal flour
1 tbsp fine oatmeal

Preheat the oven to gas mark 4 (350° F/180° C). Cover the
plum for about 30 seconds with water that has just boiled to
loosen the skin, then gently peel it off with your fingers. Cut
the flesh into small pieces, discarding the stone, mix with the
jam and place in the bottom of a lightly buttered ramekin.
Make the crumble topping by rubbing as much butter into
the flour and oatmeal as needed to get a crumbly texture,
sprinkle over the plum mixture, then bake in the centre of the
oven for about 25 to 30 minutes, or until golden on top.

To serve: Serve hot or cold. For younger babies, purée to the
desired texture with an electric/hand blender, or mash/chop
as necessary, adding a little milk or water if a thinner
consistency is required. For older babies, serve as it is with
natural unsweetened yoghurt, or ice-cream if baby's appetite
demands it.
To store: This dish may be stored in the refrigerator for up to
24 hours, or frozen for up to 1 month.

DRIED FRUIT SALAD
Cooking time: 15 minutes   *Calories: 140 (approx.)*

2 moisturised and ready-to-eat dried figs
2 moisturised and ready-to-eat dried apricots
2 moisturised and ready-to-eat pitted prunes
2 tsp ground almonds
Natural unsweetened yoghurt (optional)

Wash the fruit in a sieve under running cold water, then put it
into a small saucepan with just enough cold water to cover it.
Bring to the boil, lower the heat, cover with a fitting lid and
simmer for about 15 minutes, or until the fruit is plump and
tender, then drain, reserving the cooking liquid. Purée the
fruit and almonds until smooth with an electric/hand
blender, adding as much of the cooking liquid as necessary to
achieve a creamy consistency.

To serve: For all babies, serve hot or cold as it is, stirred with a
little natural yoghurt, if liked.
To store: This dish may be stored in the refrigerator for up to
24 hours or frozen for up to 1 month. Always add the
required amount of yoghurt just before serving.

BAKED PEACH CUSTARD
Cooking time: 30 – 40 minutes   Calories: 200 (approx.)

1 peach
3 fl oz (85ml) milk
1 size 2 egg

Preheat the oven to gas mark 3 (325°F/170°C). Cover the
peach with boiling water for a minute or two to loosen the
skin, then carefully peel it off with your fingers. Slice the flesh
into segments, discarding the stone. Purée all the ingredients
with an electric blender until smooth. Transfer to 2 lightly
buttered ramekins and bake in the centre of the oven for 30 to
40 minutes, or until a knife inserted halfway between the
centre and side of the custard comes out clean. (If the custard
is not quite cooked in the middle, the heat already present will
be sufficient to finish the cooking; taking it out at this stage
prevents overcooking.)

To serve: For all babies, serve as it is, hot or cold.
To store: This dish may be stored in the refrigerator for up to
24 hours, but should not be frozen.

CHOCOLATE MILK JELLY
Cooking time: 2 – 3 minutes   *Calories: 110 (approx.)*

4 fl oz (112ml) milk
1 tsp unrefined sugar
1 level tsp cocoa/carob powder
1 tsp gelatine

Place the milk, sugar and cocoa/carob powder in a small
milk pan and bring just up to simmering point, stirring
continuously. Remove from the heat, add the gelatine,
stirring briskly until dissolved. Rinse a small jelly mould with
cold water, pour in the jelly, allow to cool slightly then put in
the refrigerator to set. To turn the jelly out, dip the mould for
a few seconds into water that has just boiled. (This will loosen
the edges – do not leave long enough for the rest of the jelly to
start melting.)

To serve: For younger babies, mash a little if the consistency
is not liked, otherwise for all babies, serve as it is.
To store: This dish may be stored in the refrigerator for up to
24 hours, but should not be frozen.

BLACKCURRANT AND APPLE BAKE WITH
MIXED NUT TOPPING
Cooking time: 25 – 30 minutes   *Calories: 210 (approx.)*

2 tsp 'no added sugar' blackcurrant jam
¼ medium cooking apple, peeled, cored and grated

For topping
1 tbsp ground almonds
1 tbsp ground hazelnuts
1 tbsp desiccated coconut
A little butter

Preheat the oven to gas mark 4 (350° F/180° C). Mix the jam

and apple together and place in a lightly buttered ramekin.
Mix the nuts and coconut together and sprinkle over the jam.
Top with a few small dots of butter and bake in the centre of
the oven for about 25 minutes or until the apple is cooked.

To serve and to store: As for Plum and Raspberry Crumble,
page 171.

ORANGE JUICE JELLY
No cooking   *Calories: 35 (approx.)*

2 fl oz (56ml) water, boiling
1 tsp gelatine
2 fl oz (56ml) orange juice

Pour the boiling water into a small bowl and add the gelatine,
stirring briskly until dissolved, then stir in the orange juice.
Rinse a small jelly mould out with cold water, pour in the
jelly, allow to cool slightly, then put in the refrigerator to set.
To turn the jelly out, dip the mould for a few seconds into
water that has just boiled. (This will loosen the edges – do not
leave long enough for the rest of the jelly to start melting.)

To serve: For younger babies, mash a little if the consistency
is not liked, otherwise, for all babies, serve as it is.
To store: This dish may be stored in the refrigerator for up to
24 hours, but should not be frozen.

PEANUT BUTTER AND BANANA PURÉE
No cooking   *Calories: 165 (approx.)*

1 tbsp smooth peanut butter
1 very small banana
Natural unsweetened yoghurt

Mash the peanut butter and banana to a smooth texture with

a fork, adding as much yoghurt as necessary to get the right consistency.

To store: This dish is best freshly made as required.

18. BEVERAGES

FRESH LEMONADE

Makes about ½ pint (285ml)

No cooking

Calories: 20 (approx.)

The juice of 1 lemon
6 fl oz (170ml) cold water
Apple juice

Mix the lemon juice and water, then sweeten with a little apple juice to taste.

To store: This drink may be stored in the refrigerator for up to 24 hours.

SUMMER FAVOURITE

Makes 1 small cup

No cooking

Calories: 70 (approx.)

1 small peach, skin removed
2 rounded tbsp natural unsweetened yoghurt
2 tbsp pineapple juice

Purée all the ingredients with an electric blender until smooth.
To store: This drink is best consumed straightaway.

MANGO AND ORANGE DELIGHT
Makes ½ pint (285ml)
No cooking   *Calories: 115 (approx.)*

1 small mango
5 fl oz (142ml) orange juice

Cut a thick lengthways slice from each side of the fruit as close to the stone as possible. Scoop out the flesh with a spoon, then peel the centre section and carefully cut the rest of the flesh away from the stone. Purée with the orange juice using an electric blender, until smooth.
To store: This drink may be stored in the refrigerator for up to 24 hours.

BANANA MILK-SHAKE
Makes 1 small cup
No cooking   *Calories: 65 (approx.)*

½ small ripe banana
2 fl oz (56ml) milk
1 – 2 drops natural vanilla essence (optional)

Purée all the ingredients with an electric blender until smooth.
To store: This drink should be consumed straightaway.

THE GREAT REVIVER
Makes 1 small cup
No cooking   *Calories: 165 (approx.)*

1 size 2 egg yolk
1 tsp runny honey
4 fl oz (112ml) warm milk
2 drops natural vanilla essence

Purée all the ingredients with an electric blender until smooth.
To store: This drink is best consumed straightaway.

STRAWBERRY SENSATION
                                    Makes 1 small cup
No cooking   *Calories: 70 (approx.)*

3 large strawberries
1 rounded tbsp natural unsweetened yoghurt
2 fl oz (56ml) milk

Purée all the ingredients with an electric blender until smooth.
To store: This drink is best consumed straightaway.

FRESH APPLE AND ORANGE SQUASH
                            Makes about 1 pint (½ litre)
No cooking   *Calories: 80 (approx.)*

½ pint (285ml) cold water
1 dessert apple, peeled, cored and sliced
1 orange, peeled, divided into segments and any pips removed

Purée all the ingredients together with an electric blender.
To store: This drink may be stored in the refrigerator for up to 24 hours.

NUTTY MILK   Makes 1 small cup
No cooking   *Calories: 130 (approx.)*

2 tbsp ground hazelnuts or almonds
3 fl oz (85ml) milk
1 tsp runny honey
Tiny sprinkle of cinnamon
2 drops natural vanilla essence

Purée all the ingredients with an electric blender until smooth.
To store: This drink is best consumed straightaway.

KIWI COCKTAIL
No cooking

Makes 1 small cup
Calories: 60 (approx.)

1 kiwi fruit
1 satsuma orange

Cut the kiwi fruit into quarters, lengthwise. Using a sharp knife, peel off the skin carefully and discard, then gently scrape away the seeds. Peel the orange and divide into segments. Purée the flesh of both fruits with an electric blender until smooth.
To store: This drink may be stored in the refrigerator for up to 24 hours.

HOT CHOCOLATE
Cooking time: a few minutes

Makes 1 small cup
Calories: 120 (approx.)

½ tsp cocoa/carob powder
4 fl oz (112ml) milk
1 heaped tbsp skimmed milk powder
½ tsp runny honey/unrefined sugar

Put all the ingredients into a small saucepan. Bring just to the boil, stirring continuously, then remove from the heat and serve.
To store: This drink is best consumed straightaway.

ICED CHOCOLATE
No cooking

Makes 1 small cup
Calories: 90 (approx.)

½ tsp cocoa/carob powder
4 fl oz (112ml) cold milk

Iced Chocolate—contd.

2 drops natural vanilla essence
½ tsp runny honey/unrefined sugar

Purée all the ingredients with an electric blender until smooth.

To store: This drink is best consumed straightaway.

19. FINGER FOODS

Finger foods for baby to pick up and feed himself may be gradually introduced from the age of about 6 months. Instructions on how to prepare basic foods as finger foods are given below.

CEREALS

Type of cereal	Method of preparation
Dry instant wholegrain breakfast cereals e.g. Allinson's Crunchy Bran	Softened in a little milk and cut into bite-size pieces if necessary
Wholewheat pasta shapes e.g. shells and twists	Cooked and drained
Wholemeal bread	Thinly sliced and spread with a little butter, softened in milk, if necessary, and cut into bite-size pieces

Pieces of dry Instant breakfast cereal and bread can be served without being moistened once baby is chewing his food up well before swallowing it!

FRUIT

Type of fruit	*Method of preparation*
Apricots	Skin removed, de-stoned and cut into bite-size pieces
Moisturised and ready-to-eat dried apricots	Stewed and cut into bite-size pieces
Avocado pear	Skin and stone removed and cut into bite-size pieces
Banana	Peeled and cut into bite-size pieces
Moisturised and ready-to-eat dried figs	Stewed and cut into bite-size pieces
Grapefruit	Peeled, pips and pith removed and cut into bite-size pieces
Mango	Peeled, de-stoned and cut into bite-size pieces
Orange	Peel, pips and pith removed and cut into bite-size pieces
Nectarine	Skin removed, de-stoned and cut into bite-size pieces
Peach	Skin removed, de-stoned and cut into bite-size pieces
Dessert pear	Peeled, cored and cut into bite-size pieces
Dessert plum	Skin removed, de-stoned and cut into bite-size pieces
Moisturised and ready-to-eat pitted prunes	Stewed and cut into bite-size pieces
Raisins	Stewed
Raspberries	As they are
Sultanas	Stewed
Strawberries	Cut into bite-size pieces
Tomato	Raw, skins removed and cut into bite-size pieces

Once baby is used to eating fruit as a finger food try offering:

– unpeeled apricot, nectarine, peach, pear, plum, tomato

and seedless grapes to see if baby objects to eating the skin. If he doesn't, stop removing them; if he does, try again in a few weeks' time.

- larger pieces of fruit and encourage baby to try and bite off mouth-size pieces himself. He will probably try to cram the whole lot in at first, but will eventually learn that smaller bits are easier to manage.

- uncooked, moisturised and ready-to-eat dried figs, apricots and prunes; raisins and sultanas; and pieces of pineapple, once baby is chewing his food up well before swallowing it!

Hard fruits such as dessert apple should not be offered (unless grated first) until baby has the ability (i.e. plenty of teeth) and the willingness to grind them up properly before attempting to swallow them. Bits of hard fruit swallowed in lumps can cause choking.

VEGETABLES

The following vegetables should all be cooked and cut into bite-size pieces: asparagus, aubergine, green beans, dried beans, beetroot, broccoli, Brussels sprouts, cabbage, carrot, cauliflower, celery, courgette, leek, parsnip, potato, spinach, spring greens, and swede. Lentils and peas should be cooked; button mushrooms should be cooked and thinly sliced.

Once baby is used to eating vegetables as finger foods try offering:

- larger pieces of vegetables and encourage baby to try and bite off mouth-size pieces himself.

Hard vegetables such as uncooked celery should not be offered (unless grated first) until baby has plenty of teeth to be able to grind them up properly before attempting to swallow them.

MEAT, FISH AND EGGS

Type of food	Method of preparation
Minced beef, lamb or veal	Cooked
Stewing beef, veal or lamb	Cooked and finely chopped
Chicken and turkey	As above
Liver	As above
Kidney	As above
White fish	Cooked and cut into bite-size pieces
Tinned fish	Well drained and flaked, or cut into small pieces
Eggs	Medium-boiled and cut into small pieces

Meat, fish and eggs can gradually be offered in larger pieces as baby shows that he is both capable and willing to chew them up properly before swallowing.

DAIRY FOODS

Cheddar and other types of cheese which the family eats can gradually be introduced to baby. Offerings should take the form of grated cheese, or very thin slithers at first, with a gradual progression to bite-size pieces and then to larger pieces for baby to try and bite off mouth-size pieces himself.

SANDWICHES

This is also the time when you can start to give baby sandwiches. These should be made with thinly sliced wholemeal bread, crusts removed and cut into ½ inch (1cm) squares. They can be soaked in milk to moisten them a little if baby finds them too dry. Some ideas for fillings are given below, but you can probably think of many more:

Single fillings

Cheese (grated or thinly sliced), cottage cheese, 'no added sugar' jam, honey, peanut butter, egg (mashed), meat (very thinly sliced), fish (mashed), Marmite (very thinly spread), and tomato (very thinly sliced).

Combination fillings
Cheese and Marmite; cheese and tomato; cheese and cucumber; cottage cheese and 'no added sugar' jam; peanut butter and banana; peanut butter and 'no added sugar' jam; peanut butter and honey; peanut butter and grated apple; fish and tomato; fish and cucumber; egg and Marmite.

As with all other finger foods, you can gradually offer larger sandwiches for baby to bite off mouth-size pieces for himself. Other recipes for finger foods are featured in Chapters 9 to 17 (inclusive).

INDEX

Words and numbers in italics refer to actual recipes, including the fruit and vegetable purées.

A

Alcohol, 22
Allergy, 18, 37
Aluminium foil, 44
Amino acids, 12
Animal fats, 12, 14
Apple And Orange Squash, Fresh, 178
Fool, 169
Apples, 32, 49, 54, *70–71*, 183
Apricots, 13, 15, 32, 49, 54, *71–2*, 182
Ascorbic acid, 14
Asparagus, 54, *82*, 183
Aubergines, 54, *72*
Avocado pears, 49, 54, *72–3*, 182
Savoury, 157

B

Baby cereals, 11
  rice, 66
Baked Cheese Custard, 125
  Special, 122
  Egg, 118
    Custard, 168–9
  Liver Loaf, 148–9
  Peach Custard, 172
Baking powder, 52
Banana Milk Shake, 177
Bananas, 11, 16, 32, 49, *73*, 182
Beans, dried, 11, 13, 51, *83*, 183
  , green, 33, 54, *82–3*, 183
Beef, Beans And Pasta, 163–4
  Hotpot, 145
  Stew, 142
Beetroot, 33, 50, *84*, 183
Berry purée, *74*

Beverages, 57, 176 *et seq.*
Bibs, 38, 45
Bilberries, *74*
Biotin, 13
Biscuits, 11
Black Cherry Cheesecake, 170
Blackberries, *74*
Blackcurrant And Apple Bake With Mixed Nut Topping, 173–4
Blackcurrants, 14, *74*
Bread, 11, 13, 49
Breakfast Cocktail, 108
Breakfasts, 104 *et seq.*
Broccoli, 14, 15, 33, 54, *84–5*, 183
Brush, 44
Brussels sprouts, 33, 54, *85*, 183
Butter, 12, 33, 51, 53, 56
  Bean And Onion Soup, Pressure-Cooked, 113

C

Cabbage, 15, 33, 54, *86*, 183
Cakes, 11
Calcium, 14, 15
Calories, 10, 17, 34
Carbohydrates, 9 *et seq.*
Carob powder, 15, 51
Carotene, 13
Carrot And Parsley Cream, 159
  Special, 156–7
Carrots, 13, 33, 54, *86–7*, 183
Casserole, 43
Cauliflower, 16, 33, 54, *87*, 183
  With Cheese Sauce, 152–3
Celery, 54, *87–8*, 183
Cellulose, 10

Cereal products, 11, 14, 32, 48, 49, *69–70*, 181
Cheddar Fool, 129
  Salad 1, 128
    2, 129
Cheese, 15, 33, 53, 56, *102–3*, 184
  And Cucumber Purée, 123
    Soup, Cold, 114
    Potato Bake, 128
    Tomato Pie, 124
      Pizza, 123
  Custard, Baked, 125
  grater, 42
  On Beans On Toast, 106
  Special, Baked, 122
Cheesy Riceburgers, 160
  Tuna Mash, 126–7
  Vegetables, Pressure-Cooked, 126
Cherries, 49, 54, *74–5*
Chicken And Apricots, 147
  Rice, Special, 140–1
  Casserole, 149
  Salad, Cold, 141
Chilli Con Carne With Rice, Mock, 165–6
Chlorine, 15, 16
Chocolate, Hot, 179
  , Iced, 179–80
  Milk Jelly, 173
Choking, 37
Chromium, 15
Citrus fruits, 14
Cobalt, 15
Cocoa, 15, 51
Coffee, 22
Colander, 42
Cold Cheese And Cucumber Soup, 114
  Chicken Or Turkey Salad, 141
Colours, 10
Confectionery, 11
Cooked food, 47
Copper, 15
Corn, 54

Cornflour, 66
Cottage cheese, 56, *103*
    Salad 1, 127
      2, 127
  Loaf, 123–4
  Pear, 125
Courgette, 33, 54, *88*, 183
  With Cheese And Tomato, 156
Cranberries, *14*
Cream of Swede Soup, 110–11
Creamy Spinach Soup, 112
Cucumbers, 54
Currant purée, 74
Cups, 45

D
Dairy foods, 12 *et seq.*, 33, 55, *102 et seq.*, 184
Desserts, 57, 59, *168 et seq.*
Dietary fibre, *9 et seq.*
Disaccharides, 10
Dishes, 44–45
Double saucepan, 43
Dried beans, 11, 13, 15, 51, 183
  fruit, 15, 16, 50
    Salad, 171–2
  vegetables, 51
Drinks, 26, 36, 57, 176 *et seq.*
  , soft, 11

E
Egg And Bean Dinner, 119–20
    Cheese Bake, 120
    Marmite Toast, 121
    Tomato Purée, 118
    Tuna Bake, 121
    Tuna Spaghetti, 166–7
  , Baked, 118
  , Cheese and Tomato Savoury, 120
  Custard, Baked, 168–9
  dished, *117 et seq.*
  En Cocotte, 117
Eggs, 12 *et seq.*, 33, 51, 53, 55, 57, 59, 61, *101–2*, 184
Eggy Mash, 119

Electric blender, 40 *et seq.*
Energy, 9 *et seq.*
Equipment, 40 *et seq.*

F
Face-cloths, 45, 46
Fat, 9
Fats, 9 *et seq.*, 32
Fibre, dietary, 9 *et seq.*
Fifteen-Minute Rice Pudding, 170
Figs, *75–6*, 182
Finger foods, 34, 63, 181 *et seq.*
Fish, 12 *et seq.*, 33, 51, 53, 55, 57, 59, *100–1*, 184
    And Sweetcorn Soup, 115–6
        Tomato, Foil-Baked, 131
    Bake, James's Favourite, 131
    Dinner, Pressure-Cooked, 135–6
    , Saucy, 136–7
    dishes, *130, et seq.*
    Florentine, 133–4
    In Parsley Sauce, 137–8
        Savoury Custard, 133
    liver oils, 13, 14
    , tinned, 15, 51, 184
    With Cheesy Crumble Topping, 132–3
Fisherman's Pie, 132
Flavours, 10
Flour, 11, 13
Fluorine, 15
Foil-Baked Fish And Tomato, 131
    Kidney and Tomato, 150
Folic acid, 13
Food, components of, 9
    , cooked, 47
    , definition of, 9
    groups chart, 32–3
    , reheating, 46
    storage, 48 *et seq.*
Forks, 44, 45
Freezer, 58, 59
Freezing food, 59, 60, 61
French Toast, 107

Fresh Apple And Orange Squash, 178
    Lemonade, 176
    Pear Yoghurt, 168
    Tomato Soup, 111
Fried food, 22
Fructose, 10
Fruit, 10, 11, 13, 14, 16, 32, 49, 50, 53, 54, 58, 182–3
    juices, 11, 26, 38, 57
    purées, 70 *et seq.*

G
Galactose, 10
Gelatine, 51
Glucose, 10
Gooseberries, 74
Goulash, 143–4
Grape purée, 76
Grapefruit, 54, 76, 182
Grated Pear, 108
Great Reviver, The, 177–8
Greens, 54, *92–3*, 183

H
Ham, 51
Herbs, 52
High-chair, 44
Honey, 11, 22, 51
Hot Chocolate, 179
Household milk, 22, 25

I
Iced Chocolate, 179–80
Illness, 20
Iodine, 15
Iron, 14, 15, 17

J
James's Favourite Fish Bake, 131
Jelly, Chocolate Milk, 173
    , Orange Juice, 174
Juice squeezer, 44

K
Kidney, 13, 15, *97 et seq.*, 184

And Tomato, Foil-Baked, 150
Stew, 144
Kiwi Cocktail, 179
fruit, 49, 54
Knife, 44

L
Lactose, 10
Lamb And Bean Stew, 149–50
Curry With Rice, Mock, 164–5
Lard, 12
Leek And Potato Soup, 113
Leeks, 50, 88–9, 183
Left-Over Omelette, 107–8
Lemonade, Fresh, 176
Lemons, 54
Lentil Soup, 110
Supreme, 155
Lentils, 15, 51, 89–90, 183
Lettuce, 54
Limes, 54
Liver, 13 et seq., 97 et seq., 184
And Onion Casserole, 148
Swede Special, 147
Vegetables, 139–40
Loaf, Baked, 148–9
Pâté, 143
Loganberries, 74

M
Macaroni Cheese, 162
Magnesium, 14
Maltose, 10
Manganese, 15
Mango And Orange Delight, 177
Mangoes, 13, 16, 32, 49, 54, 77, 182
Margarine, 12 et seq.
Marmite, 15, 52
Measuring jug, 43
Meat, 12 et seq., 33, 51, 53 et seq., 59, 97 et seq., 184

Dinner, Pressure-Cooked, 141–2
dishes, 139 et seq.
, red, 12
Melons, 50, 77
Milk, 11, 14, 15, 17, 33, 53, 56
, household, 22, 26
, Nutty, 178–9
Shake, Banana, 177
Milky Potatoes With Cheese, 153
Mince, 184
And Parsnip Bake, 145–6
Minerals, 9, 10, 11, 14 et seq.
Minestrone Soup, 115
Mixed Root Mash, 154
Vegetable Bake With Optional Crumble Topping, 158
Mock Chilli Con Carne With Rice, 165–6
Lamb Curry With Rice, 164–5
Monosaccharides, 10
Monounsaturated fatty acids, 11
Muesli, 105
Mulberries, 74
Mushrooms, 54, 90, 183

N
Nectarines, 49, 54, 78, 182
Niacin, 13
Nutrients, 9, 17
Nutrition, 9 et seq.
Nuts, 12 et seq., 32, 52
Nutty Milk, 178–9

O
Oat And Apple Breakfast, 106
Omelette, Left-Over, 107–8
Onions, 50
Orange Juice Jelly, 174
Oranges, 16, 32, 54, 76, 182

P
Pantothenic acid, 13

Pantry, 48
Parsnips, 33, 54, *90–1*, 183
Pasta, 49
    dishes, *162 et seq.*
Pastries, 11
Pâté, Liver, 143
'Patience-preserver', 63
Pea Soup, Thick, 114
Peach Custard, Baked, 172
Peaches, 16, 32, 49, 54, 78, 182
Peanut Butter And Banana
        Purée, 174–5
            sandwiches, 13
Pear Yoghurt, Fresh, 168
Pears, 33, 49, 54, 58, *78*, 108,
    182
Peas, 11, 13, 15, 51, 54, *91*, 183
Peppers, 14, 54
Phosphorous, 14, 15
Pineapples, 50, 78–9
Plum And Raspberry Crumble,
    171
    Tomato Scramble, 104
Plums, 33, 49, 54, *79*, 182
Polysaccharides, 10
Polyunsaturated fatty acids, 11,
    12
Porridge And Banana, 105
Potassium, 15, 16
Potato peeler, 44
Potatoes, 11, 14 *et seq.*, 33, 50,
    91–2, 183
Poultry, 15, 53–4, 59, *97 et seq.*
Pressure-Cooked Butter Bean
    And
        Onion Soup, 113
        Cheesy Vegetables, 126
        Fish Dinner, 135–6
        Meat Dinner, 141–2
Pressure cooker, 43
Proteins, 9, 10, 12
Prunes, *80*, 182
Purées, 18, 23, 26 *et seq.*, 56, 59,
    69 *et seq.*
Pyridoxine, 13

R
Raisins, *80–1*, 182

Ramekin, 43
Raspberries, *74*, 182
Ratatouille, 157
Redcurrants, *74*
Refrigerator, 52–3
Reheating food, 47, 61
Rhubarb, *81*
Riboflavin, 13
Rice, 13 *et seq.*
    , baby, 66
    , brown, 11
    dishes, 160 *et seq.*
    Pudding, Fifteen-Minute, 170
    , white, 11
Risotto, Special, 167

S
Salmon, 15
    Kedgeree, 161
    Salad, Simple, 130
Salmonella, 61
Salt, 18, 21, 63
Sandwiches, 38, 184
Sardine And Carrot Loaf, 134
Sardines, 15
Saturated fatty acids, 11
Saucepans, 42–3
Saucy Fish Dinner, 136–7
Scotch Broth, 109–10
Selenium, 15
Sharon Fruit Delight, 169
Shepherd's Pie, 146
Sieve, 42
Simple Salmon Salad, 130
Skimmed milk powder, 52
Sodium, 14, 16
Soups, 57, 59, 109 *et seq.*
Soya beans, 12
Spaghetti Bolognese, 162–3
Spatula, 44
Special Risotto, 167
Speedy Beany, 153
Spices, 16, 52, 63
Spinach, 13, 15, 33, 54, *92*, 183
    Scramble, 118–9
    Soup, Creamy, 112
Spoons, 45
Sprouts, 14, 33, 54, *85*, 183

Squash, winter, 50
Starches, 10
Steamed Egg, 117
Storage of food, 48 *et seq.*
Storecupboard, 48
Strainer, 42
Strawberries, 58, *74*, 182
Strawberry Sensation, 178
Stuffed Baked Potato, 154
Sucrose, 10
Sugar, 21, 52, 63
Sugars, 10, 11
Sultanas, 16, *80–1*, 182
Summer Favourite, 176–7
  *Vegetable Casserole,
  151–2*
Sunrise Yoghurt, 107
Swede, 50, *93–4*, 183
  Soup, Cream Of, 110–11
Sweet potatoes, 13, *91–2*

T
Tap water, 22
Tea, 22
Tea-Time Special, 136
Thawing food, 61
Thiamin, 13
Thick Pea Soup, 114
Tinned food, 57
  fruit, 50
  vegetables, 50
Tomato purée, 52
  Rice With Cheese, 161
  Soup, Fresh, 111
Tomatoes, 13, 16, 50, 54,
  81–2, 182
Travelling, 38–9
Tuna Salad, 135
Turkey Salad, Cold, 141
Turnips, 50, *94*

V
Vegetable Bake, Mixed, 158
  Broth, *111–12*
  Casserole, Summer, 151
    Winter, 155
  dishes, *150 et seq.*
  juices, 11
  oils, 12, 14
  purées, *82 et seq.*
Vegetables, 10, 11, 13 *et seq.*,
  33, 50, 51, 53, 54, 58
Vegetarians, 13, 32
Vitamins, 9, 10, 11, 13, 14

W
Water, 9, 10, 22
Watercress, 13, 15
Weaning, 17
  guide, 25 *et seq.*
Wheatgerm, 66
White bread, 11
  flour, 11
Wholegrain cereals, 11 *et seq.*,
  48
Wholemeal bread, 11, 14, 15, 32
  flour, 11, 14, 15, 49
*Winter Vegetable Casserole,
  155*

Y
Yams, 11
Yeast extract, 14, 15
Yoghurt, 33, 53, 56, *103*
  , *Fresh Pear, 168*
  , *Sunrise, 107*

Z
Zinc, 15

OUR PUBLISHING POLICY

HOW WE CHOOSE

Our policy is to consider deserving manuscripts and we can give special editorial help where an author is an authority on his subject but an inexperienced writer. We are rigorously selective in the choice of books we publish. We set the highest standards of editorial quality and accuracy. This means that a *Paperfront* is easy to understand and delightful to read. Where illustrations are necessary to convey points of detail, these are drawn up by a subject specialist artist from our panel.

HOW WE KEEP PRICES LOW

We aim for the big seller. This enables us to order enormous print runs and achieve the lowest price for you. Unfortunately, this means that you will not find in the *Paperfront* list any titles on obscure subjects of minority interest only. These could not be printed in large enough quantities to be sold for the low price at which we offer this series. We sell almost all our *Paperfronts* at the same unit price. This saves a lot of fiddling about in our clerical departments and helps us to give you world-beating value. Under this system, the longer titles are offered at a price which we believe to be unmatched by any publisher in the world.

OUR DISTRIBUTION SYSTEM

Because of the competitive price, and the rapid turnover, *Paperfronts* are possibly the most profitable line a bookseller can handle. They are stocked by the best bookshops all over the world. It may be that your bookseller has run out of stock of a particular title. If so, he can order more from us at any time—we have a fine reputation for "same day" despatch, and we supply any order, however small (even a single copy), to any bookseller who has an account with us. We prefer you to buy from your bookseller, as this reminds him of the strong underlying public demand for *Paperfronts*. Members of the public who live in remote places, or who are housebound, or whose local bookseller is unco-operative, can order direct from us by post.

FREE

If you would like an up-to-date list of all paperfront titles currently available, send a stamped self-addressed envelope to
ELLIOT RIGHT WAY BOOKS, BRIGHTON RD.,
LOWER KINGSWOOD, SURREY, U.K.